JOHN ADAMS

The Writer

JOHN ADAMS
—The Writer—

A Treasury of Letters, Diaries, and Public Documents

Compiled and Edited by Carolyn P. Yoder

CALKINS CREEK
HONESDALE, PENNSYLVANIA

Copyright © 2007 by Carolyn P. Yoder
All rights reserved

Calkins Creek
An Imprint of Boyds Mills Press, Inc.
815 Church Street
Honesdale, Pennsylvania 18431
Printed in China

CIP data is available.

First edition
The text of this book is set in 12-point Goudy.

10 9 8 7 6 5 4 3 2 1

COVER: American artist John Singleton Copley (1738–1815) painted this oil portrait of John Adams in 1783, when Adams was in his late forties.

To my sister, Charlotte, whose love of John and
Abigail inspired me

TEXT CREDITS

All quotations and excerpts are from the printed volumes of Adams's writings edited by Charles Francis Adams (see p. 135) except the following:

From *The Adams-Jefferson Letters: The Complete Correspondence Between Thomas Jefferson and Abigail and John Adams* edited by Lester J. Cappon. Copyright © 1959 by the University of North Carolina Press, renewed 1987 by Stanley B. Cappon. Used by permission of the publisher. www.uncpress.unc.edu: 116 (October 7, 1818, letter excerpts), 117.

Courtesy of the **Massachusetts Historical Society:** John Adams to his grandsons, George Washington Adams and John Adams 2d, 3 May 1815. Adams Family Papers: 14; John Adams to John Quincy Adams, 14 May 1781. *Adams Family Correspondence. Vol. 4, October 1780–September 1782*, p. 114: 16; Butterfield, L. H., ed. *Adams Family Correspondence, Vol. 1, December 1761–May 1776*. Cambridge, MA: The Belknap Press of Harvard University, 1963, pgs. 2, 45–46: 25 (top and bottom); Butterfield, L. H., and Marc Friedlaender, eds. *Adams Family Correspondence, Vol. 3, April 1778–September 1780*. Cambridge, MA: The Belknap Press of Harvard University Press, 1973, pgs. 181–182: 55.

Schutz, John A., and Douglass Adair, eds. *The Spur of Fame: Dialogues of John Adams and Benjamin Rush, 1805–1813*. Indianapolis: Liberty Fund, 1966: 112 (August 20, 1811, letter excerpts).

PICTURE CREDITS

National Park Service, **Adams National Historical Park:** 14, 56, 57, 63, 79, 80, 87, 89, 98, 114, 117, 122, 134 (top), 135.

Boston Athenaeum: 13.

Grafton, John. *The American Revolution: A Picture Sourcebook*. New York: **Dover Publications, Inc.,** 1975: 26, 27, 32, 35, 36, 55, 69, 73, 97.

Fenimore Art Museum, Cooperstown, New York; Photo credit: Richard Walker: 40, 119.

The Granger Collection, New York: 95.

Independence National Historical Park: 11.

Courtesy of the **John Adams Library at the Boston Public Library,** Copley Square: 19, 85 (top).

Library of Congress, LC-USZ62-45523: 17; Library of Congress, Prints and Photographs Division, LC-USZ62-134241: 28; Library of Congress, Rare Book and Special Collections Division, LC-USZ62-45554: 30; Library of Congress, Prints and Photographs Division, LC-USZ62-76980: 31; Library of Congress, Prints and Photographs Division, LC-USZ62-55279: 39; Library of Congress, Prints and Photographs Division, LC-USZ62-110640: 43; Library of Congress, Prints and Photographs Division, LC-USZ62-46541: 45; Library of Congress, Prints and Photographs Division, LC-USZ62-40478: 48; Library of Congress, Prints and Photographs Division, LC-USZ62-70531: 49; Library of Congress, Prints and Photographs Division, LC-USZ62-26779: 50; Library of Congress, Prints and Photographs Division, LC-USZ6-279: 65; Library of Congress, Prints and Photographs Division, LC-USZ62-119824: 75; Library of Congress, Prints and Photographs Division, LC-USZ62-95063: 82; Library of Congress, Prints and Photographs Division, LC-USZ62-9422: 83; Library of Congress, Prints and Photographs Division, LC-USZ62-44907: 92; Library of Congress, Prints and Photographs Division, LC-USZ62-56344: 101; Library of Congress, Prints and Photographs Division, LC-USZ62-461: 103; Library of Congress, Prints and Photographs Division, LC-USZ61-432: 111; Library of Congress, Prints and Photographs Division, LC-USZ62-126310: 121 (left); Library of Congress, Prints and Photographs Division, LC-USZ62-14438: 121 (right).

K. A. Mason: 3, 24, 25, 41, 81, 124, 125, 126, 129, 130, 132, 134 (bottom), 138.

Courtesy of the **Massachusetts Historical Society:** 23.

Gilbert Stuart, *Abigail Smith Adams (Mrs. John Adams)*, Gift of Mrs. Robert Homans, Image © 2007 Board of Trustees, **National Gallery of Art,** Washington: 105 (left); Gilbert Stuart, *John Adams*, Gift of Mrs. Robert Homans, Image © 2007 Board of Trustees, National Gallery of Art, Washington: 105 (right).

North Wind Picture Archives: 37, 52, 62, 85 (bottom), 102, 107, 108, 110.

National Portrait Gallery, **Smithsonian Institution;** bequest of Charles Francis Adams; Frame conserved with funds from the Smithsonian Women's Committee: 77; National Portrait Gallery, Smithsonian Institution: 84.

Worcester Art Museum, Worcester, Massachusetts, museum purchase: 20.

ACKNOWLEDGMENTS

To Richard A. Ryerson, senior historian of The David Library of the American Revolution and past editor in chief of *The Adams Papers*, for helping me shape the text and for reviewing my words and the words of John Adams. I truly appreciate his patience and careful comments.

Also thanks to

Karen A. Mason for traveling with me to Quincy and Weymouth and for helping me "capture" all the places associated with the Adams family;

Patty Smith, museum technician, and Kelly Cobble, curator, of the Adams National Historical Park, Quincy, Massachusetts;

Arthur Ducharme, director of historic interpretive programs at United First Parish Church (Church of the Presidents), Quincy, Massachusetts;

Ginny Karlis of the Abigail Adams Birthplace, Weymouth, Massachusetts;

Ed Fitzgerald of the Quincy Historical Society, Quincy, Massachusetts;

Louis Cataldo, county archivist, for acquainting me with the history of Barnstable, Massachusetts, particularly with the life of Mercy Otis Warren;

Maura Marx of the Boston Public Library for introducing me to the actual books of John Adams;

Kimberly Nusco, reference librarian of the Massachusetts Historical Society, Boston, Massachusetts, for all her help;

The staff of The David Library of the American Revolution, Washington Crossing, Pennsylvania, for providing such a wonderful environment to read the works of John Adams edited by Charles Francis Adams; and

Mary T. Makarski for helping me proofread Adams's documents.

CONTENTS

———⊰◆⊱———

EDITOR'S NOTE

John Adams by Charles Willson Peale, from life,
about 1791-1794.

To tell John Adams's story, I relied on his printed writings edited by Charles Francis Adams in the nineteenth century. Charles Francis Adams was the son of John Quincy Adams and grandson of John Adams. An editor, lawyer, and diplomat, Charles Francis was dedicated to preserving his family's legacy. He also edited the papers of his father and his grandmother Abigail Adams.

In 1954, the Massachusetts Historical Society began *The Adams Papers*, dedicated to publishing the writings of John Adams, Abigail Adams, and four generations of the Adams family. In preparing the letters for publication, *The Adams Papers* staff provides a faithful transcription of the documents and supplies annotation. So far, more than thirty-eight volumes have been published.

INTRODUCTION

MEET JOHN ADAMS

Mather Brown (1761–1831) painted this portrait of John Adams. Born in Boston, Brown spent many years painting in England. Thomas Jefferson exchanged a Brown portrait of himself for this painting.

Whatever you write preserve.
May 3, 1815

⟫◆⟪

JOHN ADAMS WAS A MAN WITH PLENTY ON HIS MIND. He kept a diary and wrote often to family, friends, and the people he worked with. He wrote books and essays and newspaper articles—and a state constitution. But Adams didn't confine his thoughts to paper. He also liked to talk—to debate and argue. Adams was passionate about many things but mostly about the ever-changing world around him and his place in it. Also ambitious, Adams wanted to succeed in this world. He wanted his actions and words to be seen and heard—and, perhaps most of all, remembered.

Adams got off to a slow start. As a child in Braintree, Massachusetts, he often could be found outside, flying kites, sailing boats and ships on ponds, and playing marbles. Intent on being a farmer like his father, Adams did not like the local public schools. It wasn't until he attended private classes with Joseph Marsh that Adams became a lover of learning and books—"to study in

In 1849, artist G. Frankenstein painted the birthplaces of John Adams and John Quincy Adams.

earnest." His father planned on sending him to Harvard College in Cambridge, and John, at age fifteen and the eldest son, happily agreed. Alone on horseback, Adams headed off to take the Harvard entrance examination. His classes with Mr. Marsh paid off. Harvard awarded him a partial scholarship.

At Harvard, John not only studied Greek, Latin, philosophy, science, and mathematics but also formed lifelong friendships with men who were as passionate about learning and their place in the world as he was. Adams developed a "growing curiosity" at college, a trait he never lost.

Adams's first job after Harvard was teaching young men, but he found the position unrewarding and frustrating. In his early twenties, he questioned his ambitions and his future. Affected by the French and Indian War that was taking place and the political climate of the times, Adams decided to improve himself daily and study law. He read, wrote, and talked about everything from law to politics to religion.

After finishing his law studies, Adams moved to Boston, where he made sure to work with the city's leading lawyers. He was determined to succeed. Although Adams constantly questioned his abilities, he *did* succeed, handling important cases and meeting influential people. He also became caught up in the political tensions that were brewing in Boston. He played a key role in the trial of the British officer and soldiers involved in the Boston Massacre and was in the city when British tea was dumped in the harbor. Adams wrote privately about himself and the times in which he lived, but he also began to write publicly about the events in Boston, protesting Great Britain's treatment of the colonies.

It was also at this time that Adams met Abigail Smith. Like John, Abigail was smart and loved to read and write—and talk. From the time they married in 1764, they shared and discussed ideas passionately, in person but often in letters.

Adams did make a name for himself. Besides being a husband, father, and small farmer, he was a public servant and was often away from home. Adams served in local government, in two Continental Congresses, abroad as a diplomat, and as the country's first vice president and second president.

He voiced his opinions loudly—in person and on paper—and usually had little patience for those who disagreed with him or misunderstood him. As a result, Adams was not a politician—able to work well with others. But his main accomplishments are many. It was Adams who promoted independence early at the Second Continental Congress and who recommended George Washington as commander in chief of the Continental Army. It was Adams who practically wrote the Massachusetts constitution, still in effect today. It was Adams who approached the Dutch for a loan during the Revolutionary

War. It was Adams who established the positions of minister to Great Britain and U.S. vice president. It was Adams who established peace with France after the war for independence. And it was Adams who wrote often about his new country, documenting its early history.

But Adams questioned himself—sometimes unsure about the effect of his strong opinions. He was also insecure about the way he looked. Adams was overweight, only five feet seven—several inches shorter than Washington and Thomas Jefferson—pale, and bald. He was also plagued by poor health and a nasty temper.

But Adams was perhaps most insecure about his place in history—if his words and actions would be remembered. How would he compare with Benjamin Franklin, Alexander Hamilton, Washington, or Jefferson?

John Adams would be pleased to know that he is indeed remembered. His actions that helped build an independent America are evident to this day. And his words are read and enjoyed more than two hundred years after they were written—for their power and poetry.

⊰◆⊱

You will never be alone, with a Poet in your Poket.
You will never have an idle Hour.

May 14, 1781

CHAPTER ONE

MAKING A NAME FOR HIMSELF

*Honesty, sincerity, and openness I esteem essential marks
of a good mind.*

Sunday, March 7, 1756

This woodcut of Harvard shows the college after John Adams was a student there.

To Nathan Webb, October 12, 1755 (Excerpt)

Shortly after graduating from Harvard College in the summer of 1755, Adams moved to Worcester, Massachusetts, to teach grammar school. In the following letter to his Harvard classmate and distant cousin, Adams discusses the rise and fall of civilizations and predicts the growth and influence of a united America.

In 1755, the French and Indian War had just begun. France and England were fighting over land in America. For Adams, the whole town of Worcester was "immersed in politics." Politics was "the subject of every conversation." He tells his friend, "Be not surprised that I am turned politician."

Almost twenty years of age, Adams is keenly aware of the ways of the world. Little did he know that it wouldn't be all that long before he, too, would be immersed in politics.

This is one of John Adams's oldest surviving letters.

If we look into history, we shall find some nations rising from contemptible beginnings, and spreading their influence till the whole globe is subjected to their sway. When they have reached the summit of grandeur, some minute and unsuspected cause commonly effects their ruin, and the empire of the world is transferred to some other place. . . .

England, immediately upon this, began to increase (the particular and minute causes of which I am not historian enough to trace) in power and magnificence, and is now the greatest nation upon the globe. Soon after the Reformation, a few people came over into this new world for conscience sake. Perhaps this apparently trivial incident may transfer the great seat of empire into America. It looks likely to me: for if we can remove the turbulent Gallicks [the French], our people, according to the exactest computations, will in another century become more numerous than England itself. Should this be the case, since we have, I may say, all the naval stores of the nation in our hands, it will be easy to obtain the mastery of the seas; and then the united force of all Europe will not be able to subdue us. The only way to keep us from setting up for ourselves is to disunite us. . . . Keep us in distinct colonies . . .

Diary Entry, November 18, 1755

John Adams started keeping a diary as a teenager in college but became devoted to it after graduation when he was living in Worcester. Adams would keep a diary of his observations—about himself and his world—on and off throughout much of his lifetime. Reading his diaries gives us an inside look into his personality and the power of his words. They convince us that Adams was indeed a writer, a lover of language.

While visiting his family in Braintree, Massachusetts, Adams experiences a devastating earthquake that seems "to have been greater in Massachusetts than any other colony." In fact, this earthquake is still considered the strongest recorded shock to hit the East Coast of North America.

> 1755. November 18. We had a very severe shock of an earthquake. It continued near four minutes. I then was at my father's in Braintree, and awoke out of my sleep in the midst of it. The house seemed to rock and reel and crack, as if it would fall in ruins about us. Chimneys were shattered by it within one mile of my father's house.

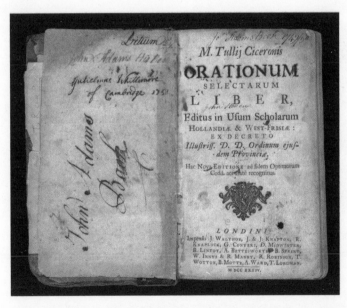

At the age of fourteen, Adams acquired this book by Cicero. Marcus Tullius Cicero was a well-known orator, philosopher, statesman, and author in ancient Rome. Adams's personal library, totaling over 3,500 books, can be found at the Boston Public Library in Massachusetts, along with a few of his letters.

DIARY ENTRY, APRIL 23, 1756

Adams did not like teaching, his young students, or life in Worcester. He found the town dull. In this diary entry, Adams doesn't know what to do with his situation and with himself. He is a frustrated twenty-year-old.

> 23. Friday. I can as easily still the fierce tempest or stop the rapid thunderbolt, as command the motions and operations of my own mind. I am dull and inactive, and all my resolutions, all the spirits I can muster are insufficient to rouse me from this senseless torpitude. My brains seem constantly in as great confusion and wild disorder as Milton's chaos; they are numb, dead. I have never any bright, refulgent ideas. Every thing appears in my mind dim and obscure, like objects seen through a dirty glass or roiled water.

Ralph Earl (1751–1801) painted *Looking East from Denny Hill* in 1800. It is probably the earliest painted view of Worcester, created about fifty years after John Adams lived there. The winding road was the original post road between Boston and New York and is now Worcester's Main Street. Shrewsbury, Massachusetts, is in the distance. Earl painted portraits but later in life turned to landscapes. The view of this landscape was taken from the family homestead of Colonel Thomas Denny, Jr., who commissioned the painting.

Diary Entry, July 21, 1756

Adams did not remain frustrated for long. He soon began to question his future and started to think of ways to improve himself. In this diary entry, written three months later, Adams is determined to spend his time more wisely, carefully studying certain authors and observing everything he sees.

Adams knew that he didn't want to devote his life to teaching. He had considered becoming a minister. His father had wanted him to be one, and he hated to go against his father's wishes. He also considered medicine. Finally, about the time he writes the following, Adams decides to become a lawyer, a profession that was becoming more and more respected. Since there were no law schools at the time, Adams arranges, in August, to read law with James Putnam, a well-known Worcester lawyer, while he continues to teach school.

> July 21. Wednesday. Kept school. I am now entering on another year, and I am resolved not to neglect my time as I did last year. I am resolved to rise with the sun, and to study the Scriptures on Thursday, Friday, Saturday, and Sunday mornings, and to study some Latin author the other three mornings. Noons and nights I intend to read English authors. This is my fixed determination; and I will set down every neglect and every compliance with this resolution. May I blush whenever I suffer one hour to pass unimproved. I will rouse up my mind and fix my attention; I will stand collected within myself, and think upon what I read and what I see; I will strive, with all my soul, to be something more than persons who have had less advantages than myself.

CHAPTER TWO

LAW, FAMILY, AND POLITICS

*Rose early, five o'clock; a pleasant morning. The more I
write the better. Writing is a most useful, improving exercise.*

Sunday, June 15, 1760

Mrs. John Adams. Pastel on paper by
Benjamin Blyth, circa 1766.

John Adams. Pastel on paper by Benjamin
Blyth, circa 1766.

But I must stay more at home, and commit more to writing. A pen is certainly an excellent instrument to fix a man's attention and to inflame his ambition. I am, therefore, beginning a new literary year in the twenty-sixth of my life.

Friday, November 14, 1760

Abigail Adams's birthplace in Weymouth, Massachusetts, is now a public museum (above and right).

To Abigail Smith, May 7, 1764 (excerpt)

In 1758, Adams left Worcester and teaching and returned home to Braintree to become a full-time lawyer. That same year he was admitted to the bar in Boston. There he was taken under the wing of Jeremiah Gridley, an established Boston lawyer, who encouraged Adams to concentrate on the law and avoid marrying early—in order to establish his reputation. Adams followed Gridley's advice. It wasn't long before he became a successful lawyer, and it took six years for him to marry.

In 1759, Adams met fourteen-year-old Abigail Smith from nearby Weymouth, Massachusetts, at a party but wasn't taken with her. He was infatuated with Hannah Quincy. Two years later, however, Abigail and

John were reintroduced, and their relationship soon became serious. Abigail, like John, was smart and curious—a good writer and avid reader.

In his first letter to Abigail, John playfully orders her "to give him, as many Kisses, and as many Hours of your Company after 9 O'Clock as he shall please to Demand and charge them to my Account." In another letter, written a few months before they married, John continues his playful tone. In answer to a letter from Abigail outlining his faults, Adams takes the opportunity to list hers. He points to her dislike of cards, her shyness, and her inability to sing and sit properly. In the following excerpt, he highlights how she walks.

At the end of the letter, Adams recognizes that Abigail does not have that many faults—that "all the rest is bright and luminous." Abigail, age nineteen, and John, age twenty-eight, were married on October 25, 1764. They enjoy each other's company for fifty-four years of marriage.

> A sixth Imperfection is that of Walking, with the Toes bending inward. This Imperfection is commonly called Parrot-toed, I think, I know not for what Reason. But it gives an Idea, the reverse of a bold and noble Air, the Reverse of the stately strutt, and the sublime Deportment.

Well-known lawyer and patriot James Otis (1725–1783) helped the young John Adams when he came to Boston. Otis's sister, Mercy Otis Warren, was also well known as a patriot and an author.

Copies of stamps used on publications.

DIARY ENTRY, DECEMBER 18, 1765 (EXCERPT)

By the middle of the 1760s, Adams was a husband, a father, a town official, and an established lawyer. He was also becoming known for his political views. Adams had written several political newspaper essays, and a few months before writing this diary entry, he published *A Dissertation on the Canon and Feudal Law*. In this work, Adams discusses how the early colonists came to America for political and religious freedom—to get away from the canon (church) and feudal laws of England. One month later, he prepared Braintree's instructions for its delegate to the General Court of Massachusetts. Both dealt with the Stamp Act. Adams, the writer, was concerned with the idea of liberty—that the colonists should have a strong say in how they were governed. At this time, the colonists were being taxed on sugar and on almost all printed matter.

Although he recognized the need to take a stand against some British laws—particularly those that taxed the colonists without representation— Adams was also concerned with how the Stamp Act with its duties on printed matter, including legal documents, hurt business, particularly his own. The courts in Boston were closed due to the Stamp Act, and Adams was out of work.

Always concerned with getting ahead, he also worried about his reputation. He needed to stay in business to achieve recognition and fame. At the end of the entry he admits, "I have groped in dark obscurity, till of late, and had but just become known and gained a small degree of reputation, when this execrable project was set on my foot for my ruin as well as that of America in general, and of Great Britain."

> The year 1765 has been the most remarkable year of my life. . . .
> The people, even to the lowest ranks, have become more attentive to their liberties, more inquisitive about them, and more determined to defend them, than they were ever before known or had occasion to be; innumerable have been the monuments of wit, humor, sense, learning, spirit, patriotism, and heroism, erected in the several colonies and provinces in the course of this year. Our presses have groaned, our pulpits have thundered, our legislatures have resolved, our towns have voted; the crown officers have everywhere trembled, and all their little tools and creatures been afraid to speak and ashamed to be seen.

Two weeks later, Adams calls for the end of the unfair taxes, particularly the Stamp Act, the one that hits closest to home.

In this Paul Revere print, British ships land in Boston in 1768. Revere was also a well-known silversmith and patriot.

Diary Entry, December 30, 1765 (excerpt)

30. Monday. We are now concluding the year 1765. Tomorrow is the last day of a year in which America has shown such magnanimity and spirit, as never before appeared in any country for such a tract of country. And Wednesday will open upon us a new year, 1766, which I hope will procure us innumerable testimonies from Europe in our favor and applause, and which we all hope will produce the greatest and most extensive joy ever felt in America, on the repeal both of the Stamp Act and Sugar Act, at least of the former.

The need for liberty was becoming popular in Boston. On January 2, 1766, Adams writes: "So triumphant is the spirit of liberty everywhere." The day before, he hints at more disagreements between England and the colonies. In less than ten years, these disagreements will erupt in war.

January 1, 1766 (excerpt)

1766. January 1. Wednesday. Severe cold, and a prospect of snow. We are now upon the beginning of a year of greater expectation than any that has passed before it. This year brings ruin or salvation to the British Colonies. The eyes of all America are fixed on the British Parliament. In short, Britain and America are staring at each other; and they will probably stare more and more for some time.

———⊰◆⊱———

The only way to compose myself and collect my thoughts, is to sit down at my table, place my Diary before me, and take my pen into my hand. This apparatus takes off my attention from other objects. Pen, ink, and paper, and a sitting posture, are great helps to attention and thinking.

Wednesday, June 27, 1770

The Boston Massacre took place on Boston's King Street, March 5, 1770.

FROM JOHN ADAMS'S AUTOBIOGRAPHY (EXCERPT), 1770

Late in life, Adams wrote his autobiography, mostly for his family, but never finished it. He refers to 1770, the year that the Boston Massacre took place, as memorable. Adams and his family lived in the city at the time when British soldiers fired on a crowd of colonists. (The British had been stationed in Boston since 1768.) Five people died and six were wounded.

Although Adams believes that British Captain Preston and the soldiers deserve a fair trial, he also realizes that many people will consider defending them unwise. He knows that it might even be dangerous. But Adams also knows that this is an important event and that by defending the soldiers he can further his reputation. Fortunately for Adams, Preston and six out of the eight soldiers are found not guilty. Adams's reputation as a skilled and fair lawyer is now widely known. Throughout his life, Adams regards this case as one of his proudest moments.

At this time I had more business at the bar than any man in the Province. My health was feeble. I was throwing away as bright prospects as any man ever had before him, and I had devoted myself to endless labor and anxiety, if not to infamy and to death, and that for nothing, except what indeed was and ought to be all in all, a sense of duty. In the evening, I expressed to Mrs. Adams all my apprehensions. That excellent lady, who has always encouraged me, burst into a flood of tears, but said she was very sensible of all the danger to her and to our children, as well as to me, but she thought I had done as I ought; she was very willing to share in all that was to come, and to place her trust in Providence. . . .

The juries in both cases, in my opinion, gave correct verdicts. It appeared to me, that the greatest service which could be rendered to the people of the town, was to lay before them the law as it stood, that they might be fully apprized of the dangers of various kinds which must arise from intemperate heats and irregular commotions. Although the clamor was very loud among some sorts of people, it has been a great consolation to me, through life, that I acted in this business with steady impartiality, and conducted it to so happy an issue.

About one year later, the front page of *The Boston Gazette* covered the Boston Massacre's anniversary.

DIARY ENTRY, MARCH 5, 1773 (EXCERPT)

Three years after the Boston Massacre, Adams attends a ceremony commemorating the event. Adams's opinion of his role in the massacre is quite clear in the following diary excerpt. But Adams, the patriot, is also proud of the role his country played.

> I have reason to remember that fatal night. The part I took in defence of Captain Preston and the soldiers procured me anxiety and obloquy enough. It was, however, one of the most gallant, generous, manly, and disinterested actions of my whole life, and one of the best pieces of service I ever rendered my country. Judgment of death against those soldiers would have been as foul a stain upon this country as the executions of the quakers or witches [at Salem] anciently. As the evidence was, the verdict of the jury was exactly right.

On December 2, 1773, Bostonians were warned about buying tea from England. Two weeks later, the Boston Tea Party took place (above).

DIARY ENTRY, DECEMBER 17, 1773 (EXCERPT)

Adams was also proud of how his countrymen acted on the night of December 16, 1773. After the Sugar Act had been revised and the Stamp Act repealed, Britain inflicted the Townshend Acts on the colonies— duties placed on certain imported goods. In 1770, most of these duties were repealed. Three years later, the British Parliament, having retained its earlier tax on tea collected in America, allowed the British East India Company to sell tea to the colonists without paying any duties in England, thereby underselling any tea smuggled in from other countries. Before this, the colonists had been boycotting tea sold by the Company.

On the evening of December 16, 1773, about sixty or so Boston residents dressed as Mohawk Indians raided three ships in Boston's harbor, throwing their crates of tea overboard. Never in favor of mob violence, Adams has nothing but praise for this peaceful and symbolic protest.

> Last night, three cargoes of Bohea [black] tea were emptied into the sea. This morning a man-of-war sails [to bring the news to England]. This is the most magnificent movement of all. There is a dignity, a majesty, a sublimity, in this last effort of the patriots, that I greatly admire. The people should never rise without doing something to be remembered, something notable and striking. This destruction of the tea is so bold, so daring, so firm, intrepid and inflexible, and it must have so important consequences, and so lasting, that I cannot but consider it as an epocha* in history.

*Epoch, or memorable event.

CHAPTER THREE

DEDICATED TO LIBERTY

I must be excused from writing a syllable of anything of any moment. My letters have been and will be nothing but trifles. I don't choose to trust the post. I am afraid to trust private travellers. They may peep. Accidents may happen. And I would avoid, if I could, even ridicule, but especially mischief.

October 10, 1775

The presentation of the Declaration of Independence by the committee who prepared it. John Adams is standing at left.

Diary Entry, June 25, 1774

ONE WEEK BEFORE WRITING THIS DIARY ENTRY, John Adams was elected by the Massachusetts House of Representatives as a delegate to the First Continental Congress in Philadelphia. Joining him would be fellow lawyers Thomas Cushing and Robert Treat Paine, and his famous older cousin, Samuel Adams.

At the end of June, Adams was away from home handling law cases, but he had plenty of time to think. Writing in his diary, Adams is unsure of his qualifications and of those of his fellow delegates and prays for divine guidance. He is also fearful about the state of the country. But Adams's commitment to the cause of liberty is evident. For Adams death would be better than defeat.

25. Saturday. Since the Court adjourned without day this afternoon, I have taken a long walk through the Neck, as they call it, a fine tract of land in a general field. Corn, rye, grass, interspersed in great perfection this fine season. I wander alone and ponder. I muse, I mope, I ruminate. I am often in reveries and brown studies. The objects before me are too grand and multifarious for my comprehension. We have not men fit for the times. We are deficient in genius, in education, in travel, in fortune, in every thing. I feel unutterable anxiety. God grant us wisdom and fortitude! Should the opposition be suppressed, should this country submit, what infamy and ruin! God forbid. Death in any form is less terrible!

John Adams's older cousin Samuel Adams (1722–1803) was one of the most well-known political activists during the time of the American Revolution.

Pennsylvania State House, later known as Independence Hall, in 1776.

To Abigail Adams, September 25, 1774

Adams was busy in Philadelphia. Eleven days before writing this letter, he confesses to his wife, "my time is totally filled from the moment I get out of bed until I return to it." Here he reflects on how his time is spent and the makeup and progress of the Congress. The First Continental Congress had been in session for about three weeks and would last for one month more.

> I would not lose the opportunity of writing to you, though I must be short. Tedious indeed is our business—slow as snails. I have not been used to such ways. We sit only before dinner. We dine at four o'clock. We are crowded with a levee [meeting] in the evening.
>
> Fifty gentlemen meeting together, all strangers, are not acquainted with each other's language, ideas, views, designs. They are, therefore, jealous of each other—fearful, timid, skittish.

To Abigail Adams, October 7, 1775 (Excerpt)

Throughout the Second Continental Congress, Adams continued to be one of the busiest delegates. He was also one of the most outspoken. To his fellow delegates Adams was an ardent patriot—committed to freedom and liberty. In the following letter to Abigail he talks about the dangerous climate of the times and the need to be cautious. He is mostly concerned with his reputation—of being falsely represented.

Adams also hints at the inevitability of a violent break with Great Britain and an independent America. Although the Revolutionary War had begun months before in Massachusetts, and George Washington had been appointed commander in chief of the Continental Army—nominated by Adams—not everyone in Congress supported independence. Some wanted peace and an end to the fight. It would take almost nine more months for the Congress to come together to prepare a declaration of independence.

Really, my dear, I have been more cautious than I used to be. It is not easy to know whom to trust in these times; and if a letter from any person in the situation I am in can be laid hold of, there are so many lies made and told about it, so many false copies taken and dispersed, and so many false constructions put, that one ought to be cautious.

The situation of things is so alarming, that it is our duty to prepare our minds and hearts for every event, even the worst. From my earliest entrance into life, I have been engaged in the public cause of America; and from first to last I have had upon my mind a strong impression that things would be wrought up to their present crisis. I saw from the beginning that the controversy was of such a nature that it never would be settled, and every day convinces me more and more. This has been the source of all the disquietude of my life. It has lain down and risen up with me these twelve years. The thought that we might be driven to the sad necessity of breaking our connection with Great Britain, exclusive of the carnage and destruction, which it was easy to see must attend the separation, always gave me a great deal of grief. And even now I would cheerfully retire from public life forever, renounce all chance for profits or honors from the public, nay, I would cheerfully contribute my little property, to obtain peace and liberty. But all these must go, and my life too, before I can surrender the right of my country to a free Constitution. I dare not consent to it. I should be the most miserable of mortals ever after, whatever honors or emoluments might surround me.

It was John Adams who recommended that George Washington serve as commander in chief of the Continental Army. This print was created in the early 1900s.

～◆～

If I could write as well as you [Abigail], my sorrow would be as eloquent as yours, but, upon my word, I cannot.

October 23, 1775

In March 1776, Abigail wrote John about the need for independence and the important role of women in the patriot cause. She wrote, "I long to hear that you have declared an independency. And, by the way, in the new code of laws which I suppose it will be necessary for you to make, I desire you would remember the ladies and be more generous and favorable to them than your ancestors. Do not put such unlimited power into the hands of the husbands. Remember, all men would be tyrants if they could. If particular care and attention is not paid to the ladies, we are determined to foment a rebellion, and will not hold ourselves bound by any laws in which we have no voice or representation." Besides being a friend and wife to John, Abigail was a smart political observer and adviser. Abigail is shown here in a painting by Mather Brown, 1785.

TO ABIGAIL ADAMS, FEBRUARY 1776 (EXCERPT)

In the following letter, Adams again points to the dangerous position he is in. He even suggests that the life of an outspoken patriot is more dangerous than that of a military man. Perhaps Adams is trying to justify the fact that he never served as an active soldier or officer.

Here Adams reveals that he wanted to be a soldier during the French and Indian War, but the closest he came was delivering a military message from Worcester to Newport, Rhode Island. By 1757, he was committed to the study of law.

Adams doesn't say why he did not pursue a military career earlier in his life, but it is quite clear that he no longer believes he is qualified for it. It's interesting that a little over a year later—August 19, 1777—Adams admits, "if I had the last four years to run over again, I certainly would" gird a sword. In the long run, Adams knew that a life in the military was noble, brave, manly, and enviable. Fortunately for him and the nation, Adams was able to serve Congress as a member of the Naval Committee and president of the Board of War, which oversaw the Continental Army.

I feel, upon some of these occasions, a flow of spirits and an effort of imagination, very like an ambition to be engaged in the more active, gay, and dangerous scenes; (dangerous, I say, but recall that word, for there is no course more dangerous than that which I am in.) I have felt such passions all my lifetime, particularly in the year 1757, when I longed more ardently to be a soldier than I ever did to be a lawyer. But I am too old, and too much worn with fatigues of study in my youth, and there is too little need, in my Province, of such assistance, for me to assume a uniform.

This statue in Quincy, Massachusetts, shows Abigail with John Quincy as they witnessed the British bombardment of Charlestown at the Battle of Bunker Hill on June 17, 1775.

To Abigail Adams, April 15, 1776 (excerpt)

During the Second Continental Congress, Adams was absent from home for months. Abigail had to run the house, manage the farm, pay the bills, and raise their four children, Abigail, John Quincy, Charles, and Thomas Boylston. Although he was far from home, Adams often thought of his children and was eager to get to know them. In this letter he is both tender and strict. Adams had definite ideas about right and wrong—and the proper way to behave. Those ideas included politics.

> I will tell them [his children], that I studied and labored to pro-cure a free constitution of government for them to solace them-selves under, and if they do not prefer this to ample fortune, to ease and elegance, they are not my children, and I care not what becomes of them. They shall live upon thin diet, wear mean clothes, and work hard with cheerful hearts and free spirits, or they may be the children of the earth, or of no one, for me.
>
> John has genius and so has Charles. Take care that they don't go astray. Cultivate their minds, inspire their little hearts, raise their wishes. Fix their attention upon great and glorious objects. Root out every little thing. Weed out every meanness. Make them great and manly. Teach them to scorn injustice, ingratitude, cowardice and falsehood. Let them revere nothing but religion, morality and liberty.
>
> Abby and Tommy are not forgotten by me although I did not mention them before. The first, by reason of her sex, requires a different education from the two I have mentioned. Of this, you are the only judge. I want to send each of my little pretty flock some present or other. I have walked over this city twenty times, and gaped at every shop, like a countryman, to find something, but could not. Ask every one of them what they would choose to have, and write it to me in your next letter. From this I shall judge of their taste and fancy and discretion.

James Sullivan (1744–1808) was active in Massachusetts politics and served as governor from 1807 to 1808. Sullivan was one of the founders of the Massachusetts Historical Society and was its first president.

TO JAMES SULLIVAN, MAY 26, 1776 (EXCERPT)

Adams was still involved in the affairs of Massachusetts while he was a delegate to the Continental Congress. In the spring of 1776, he held the position of chief justice of the Massachusetts Supreme Court and was a member of the state's Provincial Congress.

In early May, Adams proposed a resolution to the Continental Congress that would require each colony to form new governments or revise certain laws—looking toward an eventual break with Great Britain. Adams was counting on Congress to declare independence.

One month before, Adams had published his *Thoughts on Government*, which suggests how the colonies could form these new governments. In it he recommends majority rule; legislative, judicial, and executive branches; and a house of representatives, a senate, and a governor.

In the following letter to James Sullivan, a member of the Provincial Congress of Massachusetts, Adams discusses voting rights in the "state" (although it was still a province). During this time, Massachusetts was divided over independence. The western counties tended to favor independence, while the eastern counties still hoped for reconciliation. Adams calls for a "general" electoral rule, granting voting rights to male property owners over twenty-one.

Adams felt that women's "attention is so much engaged with the necessary nurture of their children, that nature has made them fittest for domestic cares" and children "have not judgment or will of their own." He also believed that men with no property "talk and vote as they are directed by some man of property, who has attached their minds to his interest." But Adams wanted the "acquisition of land easy to every member of society." That way, the majority of men—not just the wealthy few—would have a say in their government.

> Society can be governed only by general rules. Government cannot accommodate itself to every particular case as it happens, nor to the circumstances of particular persons. It must establish general comprehensive regulations for cases and persons. The only question is, which general rule will accommodate most cases and most persons.
>
> Depend upon it, Sir, it is dangerous to open so fruitful a source of controversy and altercation as would be opened by attempting to alter the qualifications of voters; there will be no end of it. New claims will arise; women will demand a vote; lads from twelve to twenty-one will think their rights not enough attended to; and every man who has not a farthing, will demand an equal voice with any other, in all acts of state. It tends to confound and destroy all distinctions, and prostrate all ranks to one common level.

To Abigail Adams, June 2, 1776 (excerpt)

In 1776, Adams started copying his letters in a blank book. He gives many reasons for this: to be a better writer, to remember what he says, and to keep track of his letters. But Adams most likely knew that what he had to say was important and should be preserved—not only for the sake of his children but also for generations to come. Later on in life, Adams would become even more concerned with how he would be remembered.

> In all the correspondence I have maintained, during a course of twenty years, at least, that I have been a writer of letters, I never kept a single copy. This negligence and inaccuracy has been a great misfortune to me on many occasions. I have now

purchased a folio book, in the first page of which, excepting one blank leaf, I am writing this letter, and intend to write all my letters to you in it, from this time forward. This will be an advantage to me in several respects. In the first place, I shall write more deliberately. In the second place, I shall be able, at all times, to review what I have written. Third, I shall know how often I write. Fourth, I shall discover by this means, whether any of my letters to you miscarry. If it were possible for me to find a conveyance, I would send you such another blank book as a present, that you might begin the practice at the same time, for I really think that your letters are much better worth preserving than mine. Your daughter and sons will very soon write so good hands, that they will copy the letters for you from your book, which will improve them, at the same time that it relieves you.

John Winthrop (1714–1779) was one of John Adams's favorite teachers at Harvard College. An accomplished astronomer, Winthrop is shown seated by a telescope.

TO JOHN WINTHROP, JUNE 23, 1776 (EXCERPT)

Congress finally moved toward independence at the end of June. Adams couldn't have been happier—as shown in this letter to his professor at Harvard, astronomer John Winthrop.

Adams's hard work had paid off. He was assigned to the committee to draft a declaration of independence along with fellow delegates Benjamin Franklin, Thomas Jefferson, Roger Sherman, and Robert R. Livingston. It was Adams who suggested that Thomas Jefferson—his good friend from Virginia—write the document. To Adams, Jefferson is the better writer.

> It is now universally acknowledged that we are and must be independent. But still, objections are made to a declaration of it. It is said that such a declaration will arouse and unite Great Britain. But are they not already aroused and united, as much as they will be? Will not such a declaration arouse and unite the friends of liberty, the few who are left, in opposition to the present system? . . .
>
> The advantages which will result from such a declaration, are, in my opinion, very numerous and very great. After that event the colonies will hesitate no longer to complete their governments. They will establish tests, and ascertain the criminality of toryism. . . .
>
> A committee is appointed to prepare a confederation of the colonies, ascertaining the terms and ends of the compact, and the limits of the Continental Constitution; and another committee is appointed to draw up a declaration that these colonies are free and independent States. And other committees are appointed for other purposes, as important. These committees will report in a week or two, and then the last finishing strokes will be given to the politics of this revolution. Nothing after that will remain but war.

TO ABIGAIL ADAMS, JULY 3, 1776 (TWO LETTERS, EXCERPTS)

On July 2, 1776, the delegates to the Continental Congress voted 12–0 in favor of independence. (New York did not vote.) Little did Adams know that the country would never stop celebrating its independence, although not on July 2, but two days later when the declaration was formally adopted.

Adams became known in Congress as the "Atlas of American Independence," after the Greek god of strength who held up the sky on his shoulders. He spent many hours delivering speeches defending the declaration and independence.

> Yesterday, the greatest question was decided, which ever was debated in America, and a greater, perhaps, never was nor will be decided among men. A resolution was passed without one dissenting colony, "that these United Colonies are, and of right ought to be, free and independent States, and as such they have, and of right ought to have, full power to make war, conclude peace, establish commerce, and to do all other acts and things which other States may rightfully do." You will see in a few days a Declaration setting forth the causes which have impelled us to this mighty revolution, and the reasons which will justify it in the sight of God and man. A plan of confederation will be taken up in a few days. . . .

> The second day of July, 1776, will be the most memorable epocha in the history of America. I am apt to believe that it will be celebrated by succeeding generations as the great anniversary festival. It ought to be commemorated, as the day of deliverance, by solemn acts of devotion to God Almighty. It ought to be solemnized with pomp and parade, with shows, games, sports, guns, bells, bonfires, and illuminations, from one end of this continent to the other, from this time forward, forevermore.

To Samuel Adams, September 17, 1776 (Excerpt)

Two months after the Declaration of Independence was adopted, Adams was part of a delegation that traveled to Staten Island to meet with Lord Richard Howe, the British admiral. The other members were Benjamin Franklin of Pennsylvania and Edward Rutledge of South Carolina. Howe was hoping that peace could be restored and that America would return "to her allegiance" to Britain. At the end of this letter to his cousin, Adams, speaking of himself in the third person, points out why that would be impossible.

> Mr. J. A. observed that all the colonies had gone completely through a revolution; that they had taken all authority from the officers of the Crown, and had appointed officers of their own, which his Lordship might easily conceive had cost great struggles, and that they could not easily go back; and that Americans had too much understanding not to know that, after such a declaration as they had made, the government of Great Britain never would have any confidence in them, or could govern them again but by force of arms.

After the peace mission, Edward Rutledge became an officer in the war. Later on, he was active in South Carolina politics and served as governor from 1798 until his death at the age of fifty in 1800.

CHAPTER FOUR

A DIPLOMAT OVERSEAS

I seldom know what to write, and when I do, I don't love to write it.
October 7, 1777

In 1781, Adams was relieved of his title as sole negotiator of treaties of peace and commerce with Great Britain. He became the head of a peace commission. This print of an unfinished painting by Benjamin West shows the American peace commissioners in 1781: John Jay, John Adams, Benjamin Franklin, Henry Laurens, and William Temple Franklin. The latter served as an aide to his grandfather, Benjamin, at this time.

TO HENRY LAURENS, DECEMBER 23, 1777 (EXCERPT)

IN NOVEMBER OF 1777, JOHN ADAMS RETURNED to Braintree—permanently, he thought. He did not plan to seek reelection to Congress, where he had been a delegate for more than three years. Adams went home to be with his family, and for financial reasons. He was deeply in debt.

Adams immediately resumed his law practice. In late November, he was in Portsmouth, New Hampshire, handling a case. While there he learned he had been appointed commissioner to France. In his letter to the president of Congress, Adams writes about his qualifications and the importance of the position.

Adams was eager to travel overseas to join fellow commissioners Benjamin Franklin and Arthur Lee and form an "official" alliance with France. France's help was needed to win the war.

> As I am deeply penetrated with a sense of the high honor which has been done me in this appointment, I cannot but wish I were better qualified for the important trust; but as congress are perfectly acquainted with all my deficiencies, I conclude it is their determination to make the necessary allowances; in the humble hope of which, I shall submit my own judgment to theirs, and devote all the faculties I have, and all that I can acquire, to their service.

John Adams replaced Silas Deane (1737–1789) as commissioner to France. Before his foreign service, Deane had represented Connecticut in the Continental Congress from 1774 to 1776.

I should have been pleased to have kept a minute journal of all that passed, in the late chases and turbulent weather; but I was so wet, and every thing and place was so wet, every table and chair was so wrecked, that it was impossible to touch a pen, or paper.

Late February 1778

———⟫•⟪———

DIARY ENTRY, FEBRUARY 27, 1778 (EXCERPT)

Adams set sail for France in mid-February 1778. With him was his ten-year-old son, John Quincy. Adams wrote in his diary about the bad weather, bad food, seasickness, and encounters with British ships—even taking one of these ships captive. But for most of the time, Adams found life aboard the frigate *Boston* "dull"—with no time for business, pleasure, or study. According to Adams, "we see nothing but sky, clouds, and sea, and then sea, clouds, and sky."

Adams was restless. Never one to be silent, he took an active role during the six-week voyage, often offering advice to Captain Samuel Tucker.

> One source of the disorders in this ship, is the irregularity of meals. There ought to be a well digested system for eating, drinking, and sleeping. At six, all hands should be called up; at eight, all hands should breakfast; at one, all hands should dine; at eight again, all hands should sup. It ought to be penal for the cook to fail of having his victuals ready punctually. This would be for the health, comfort, and spirits of the men, and would greatly promote the business of the ship.
>
> I am constantly giving hints to the captain concerning order, economy, and regularity, and he seems to be sensible of the necessity of them, and exerts himself to introduce them. He has cleared out the 'tween decks, ordered up the hammocks to be aired, and ordered up the sick, such as could bear it, upon deck for sweet air. This ship would have bred the plague or the jail fever, if there had not been great exertions, since the storm, to

wash, sweep, air, and purify clothes, cots, cabins, hammocks, and all other things, places, and persons. The captain, yesterday, went down into the cockpit and ordered up everybody from that sink of devastation and putrefaction; ordered up the hammocks, &c. This was in pursuance of the advice I gave him in the morning: "If you intend to have any reputation for economy, discipline, or any thing that is good, look to your cockpit."

Although Adams found his situation difficult, he enjoyed life in France. He wrote home in early 1779, "I never had so much trouble in my life as here, and yet I grow fat. The climate and soil agree with me. So do the cookery and even the manners of the people, of those of them at least that I converse with . . ." This German print shows French clothing and hair fashions of the 1770s.

I am so sensible of the difficulty of conveying letters safe to you, that I am afraid to write any thing more than to tell you, that after all the fatigues and dangers of my voyage and journey, I am here in health.

To Abigail, April 12, 1778

——◆——

FROM JOHN ADAMS'S AUTOBIOGRAPHY, APRIL 21, 1778 (EXCERPT)

Adams and his son landed in Bordeaux, France, on April 1, 1778. When Adams arrived in Paris a week later, joining Franklin and Lee, he already knew that a formal alliance with France had been concluded. Adams must have wondered what he would do there.

In his autobiography, Adams writes about his fellow commissioners. Kinder to Lee, Adams points out that "His manners were polite, his reading extensive, his attention to business was punctual, and his integrity without reproach." Perhaps jealous of Franklin, who was quite popular in France, he writes, "Dr. Franklin, one of my colleagues, is so generally known that I shall not attempt a sketch of his character at present. That he was a great genius, a great wit, a great humorist, a great satirist, and a great politician, is certain. That he was a great philosopher, a great moralist, and a great statesman, is more questionable."

Also, according to Adams, both were disorganized and did not get along.

Adams needed something to do. He quickly set about organizing the affairs of the commissioners. He also decided that "it is no part of my business to quarrel with anybody without cause; it is no part of my duty to differ with one party or another, or to give offence to anybody; but I must do my duty to the public, let it give offence to whom it will."

I may have said before, that public business had never been methodically conducted. There never was, before I came, a minute-book, a letter-book, or an account-book; or, if there had been, Mr. Deane and Dr. Franklin had concealed them from Mr. Lee, and they were now nowhere to be found. It was utterly impossible to acquire any clear idea of our affairs. I was now determined to procure some blank books, and to apply myself with diligence to business, in which Mr. Lee cordially joined me. To this end it was necessary to alter the course of my life. Invitations were sent to Dr. Franklin and me, every day in the week, to dine in some great or small company. I determined, on my part, to decline as many as I could of these, and attend to my studies of French, and the examination and execution of that public business which suffered for want of our attention every day.

To Count de Vergennes, February 16, 1779 (excerpt)

It wasn't long before Adams wanted to return home. He felt that only one commissioner was needed in France. He even discreetly recommended Franklin, a better-liked diplomat. It wasn't until February 12, 1779, however, that Adams's wish became official. On that date, Congress's dispatches naming Franklin minister plenipotentiary (having full power) to the Court of Louis XVI reached Paris.

The dispatches also stated that Arthur Lee retain his earlier position as a commissioner to Spain. Unfortunately, nothing was said about Adams; he was neither told to come home nor given another assignment. Upset and out of a job, Adams wanted to return home "as soon as possible." Four days later he writes France's minister of foreign affairs about being "restored to the character of a private citizen."

Adams had been in Paris less than a year.

> This masterly measure of congress, which has my most hearty approbation, and of the necessity of which I was fully convinced before I had been two months in Europe, has taken away the possibility of those dissensions which I so much apprehended. I shall not, therefore, give your Excellency any further trouble, than to take an opportunity of paying my respects, in order to take leave, and to assure you that I shall leave this kingdom with the most entire confidence in his Majesty's benevolence to the United States, and inviolable adherence to the treaties between the two powers, with a similar confidence in the good disposition of his Majesty's ministers of state and of this nation towards us, and with a heart impressed with gratitude for the many civilities which I have received in the short space I have resided here, at Court, in the city and in the country, and particularly from your Excellency.

Benjamin Franklin became the sole minister to France in 1779, representing the United States at Louis XVI's court. He is shown here at the French court in 1778.

To Abigail Adams, February 28, 1779 (Excerpt)

Two weeks later, Adams reveals his true feelings to Abigail. After sacrificing so much to get to France, Adams feels neglected and unsure of his political future.

I suppose I must write every day, in order to keep or rather to restore good Humour, whether I have any thing to say or not.

The Scaffold is cutt away, and I am left kicking and sprawling in the Mire, I think. It is hardly a state of Disgrace that I am in but rather of total Neglect and Contempt. The humane People about me, feel for my situation they say: But I feel for my Countrys situation. If I had deserved such Treatment, I should have deserved to be told so at least, and then I should have known my Duty.

After sending orders to me at five hundred Miles distance which I neither solicited, nor expected nor desired, to go to Europe through the Gulf Stream, through Thunder and Lightning, through three successive storms, and three successive Squadrons of British Men of War, if I had committed any Crime which deserved to hang me up in a Gibet [gallows] in the Face of all Europe, I think I ought to have been told what it was —or if I had proved myself totally insignificant, I think I ought to have been called away at least from a Place, where I might remain a Monument of the Want of Discernment in sending me here.

There are spies upon every word I utter, and every syllable I write. Spies planted by the English, spies planted by stock-jobbers, spies planted by selfish merchants, and spies planted by envious and malicious politicians. I have been all along aware of this, more or less, but more so now than ever. My life has been often in danger, but I never considered my reputation and character so much in danger as now. I can pass for a fool, but I will not pass for a dishonest or mercenary man. Be upon your guard, therefore. I must be upon mine, and I will.

To Abigail, February 20, 1779

TO THOMAS MCKEAN, SEPTEMBER 20, 1779 (EXCERPT)

Soon after he arrived back in Braintree in August 1779, Adams became active in state politics. As a delegate to the Massachusetts Constitutional Convention, Adams was largely responsible for writing the state's constitution. But Adams was also consumed with the affairs of the country. In the following letter to Thomas McKean, a delegate to the Continental Congress, Adams reveals his concern with—and dislike of—Benjamin Franklin, sole ambassador to France. Adams is convinced that Franklin can't really handle the job alone.

According to family tradition, John gave this locket to Abigail when he left for Europe as peace commissioner in 1779.

I presume Congress intend to appoint a secretary to the commission, and to appoint consuls for the management of commercial and maritime matters. It is highly necessary. Franklin is a wit and a humorist, I know. He may be a philosopher, for what I know. But he is not a sufficient statesman for all the business he is in. He knows too little of American affairs, of the politics of Europe, and takes too little pains to inform himself of either, to be sufficient for all these things, to be ambassador, secretary, admiral, consular agent, &c. Yet such is his name, on both sides the water, that it is best, perhaps, that he should be left there; but a secretary and consuls should be appointed to do the business, or it will not be done; or, if done, it will be by people who insinuate themselves into his confidence, without either

Adams most likely wrote the Massachusetts state constitution on this stand-up law desk.

such heads or hearts as Congress should trust. He is too old, too infirm, too indolent and dissipated, to be sufficient for the discharge of all the important duties of ambassador, board of war, board of treasury, commissionary of prisoners, &c., &c., &c., as he is at present, in that department, besides an immense correspondence and acquaintance, each of which would be enough for the whole time of the most active man in the vigor of youth.

To the President of Congress, November 4, 1779 (excerpt)

Adams was home for only three months before he was sent back to France, this time "to negotiate peace and commerce" with Great Britain. Even though Congress was in a sense making up for how they had treated him earlier that year, Adams was honored by the appointment and eager to do a good job.

As usual, Adams took his new assignment quite seriously. The war was far from over, and Adams probably knew that he might be overseas for a long time. He was prepared to leave his family and once again face rough seas and possible enemy attacks to serve his country.

Peace is an object of such vast importance, the interests to be adjusted in the negotiations to obtain it are so complicated and so delicate, and the difficulty of giving even general satisfaction is so great, that I feel myself more distressed at the prospect of executing the trust, than at the thought of leaving my country, and again encountering the dangers of the seas and of enemies. Yet, when I reflect on the general voice in my favor, and the high honor that is done me by this appointment, I feel the warmest sentiments of gratitude to congress, and shall make no hesitation to accept it, and devote myself without reserve or loss of time to the discharge of it.

—◆—

I write this on my knees, and the ship rolls so that
I write worse than common.
Late November 1779

DIARY ENTRIES, DECEMBER 28 AND 30, 1779 (EXCERPTS)

Adams traveled with two secretaries; two servants; and his two older sons, John Quincy and Charles, on the *Sensible*, the same boat that had brought him home a few months before. Although the ship was forced to make port in Spain because of a dangerous leak, it was the overland journey from Spain to France that was twice as long—almost two months—and just as difficult. It was a "journey of near five hundred leagues, in the dead of winter, through bad roads and worse accommodations of every kind."

Adams captures the one-thousand-mile trip in vivid detail.

28. Tuesday. Went from Castillan to Baamonde. The first part of the road very bad; the latter part tolerable. The whole country we have passed is very mountainous and rocky. There is here and there a valley, and here and there a farm that looks beautifully cultivated; but in general the mountains are covered with furze [shrubs], and are not well cultivated. I am astonished to see so few trees; scarce an elm, oak, or any other tree to be seen; a very few walnut trees, and a very few fruit trees.

At Baamonde we stop until to-morrow, to get a new axletree to one of our calashes [carriages]. The house where we now are is better than our last night's lodgings. We have a chamber for seven of us to lodge in. We shall lay our beds upon tables, seats, and chairs, or the floor, as last night. We have no smoke, and less dirt; but the floor was never washed, I believe. The kitchen and stable are below as usual, but in better order. The fire in the middle of the kitchen; but the air holes pierced through the tiles of the roof draw up the smoke, so that one may sit at the fire without inconvenience. The mules, hogs, fowls, and human inhabitants live, however, all together below, and cleanliness seems never to be thought of.

30. Thursday . . . I see nothing but signs of poverty and misery among the people. A fertile country, not half cultivated, people ragged and dirty, and the houses universally nothing but mire, smoke, fleas, and lice. Nothing appears rich but the churches; nobody fat but the clergy. The roads, the worst without exception that ever were passed, in a country where it would be easy to

make them very good. No symptoms of commerce, or even of internal traffic; no appearance of manufactures or industry.

We are obliged in this journey to carry our own beds, blankets, sheets, pillows, &c.; our own provisions of chocolate, tea, sugar, meat, wine, spirits, and every thing that we want. We get nothing at the taverns but fire, water, and salt. We carry our own butter, cheese, and, indeed, salt and pepper, too.

TO WILLIAM LEE, APRIL 2, 1780 (EXCERPT)

While in Paris, Adams wrote fellow diplomat William Lee about his position as negotiator of peace and about the state of America and England. The Revolutionary War still wasn't over, and peace did not seem likely.

In a letter written a few days before April 2, Adams talks about his new position: "No minister that ever existed had a more difficult and dangerous peace to make than I have."

When our enemy will wish for peace so far as to think of it in earnest, I know not. Peace concerns her more than any of the belligerent powers. America even can sustain the war, although it will be irksome and grievous, infinitely better than England. America grows more powerful, more numerous, more brave, and better disciplined every year of the war, and more independent too, both in spirit and circumstances. Their trade, it is true, does not flourish as it did, but their agriculture, arts, and manufactures increase in proportion to the decline of their trade. England is wasting away, notwithstanding the violence of her convulsive struggles, in wealth, in commerce, in manufactures, in sailors, soldiers, population, and, above all, in political consideration among the powers of Europe every day. Her reputation, which is a more durable source of power, and a more constant cause of prosperity to states as well as individuals, declines amidst all her activity, exertions, and successes. The hopes and fears of other nations are turning by degrees from her to other people, and these she will find it harder to regain than even the good will of America, which is also leaving her every day. The English nation do not seem to me to see any thing in its true light, or weigh any thing in a just balance.

TO ABIGAIL ADAMS, MAY 1780 (EXCERPT)

One month later, Adams writes Abigail about how his role as a political leader and thinker will affect future generations. This is one of his most famous letters. Adams is committed to the early shaping of America so that his sons and grandchildren will have more educational opportunities. It's interesting that the arts are to be studied only by the youngest of generations, as if they are considered a luxury and not a necessity.

Later in life, Adams comments on his own education: "At college, next to the ordinary routine of classical studies, mathematics and natural philosophy were my favorite pursuits. When I began to study law, I found ethics, the law of nations, the civil law, the common law, a field too vast to admit of many other inquiries. Classics, history, and philosophy have, however, never been wholly neglected to this day." Adams seemed to have no time for the study of the arts.

> I must study politics and war that my sons may have liberty to study mathematics and philosophy. My sons ought to study mathematics and philosophy, geography, natural history and naval architecture, navigation, commerce and agriculture, in order to give their children a right to study painting, poetry, music, architecture, statuary, tapestry and porcelain.

TO BENJAMIN FRANKLIN, OCTOBER 14, 1780 (EXCERPT)

Six months after arriving in Paris, Adams decided to travel to Amsterdam in the Netherlands to negotiate a loan. Adams did not get along with Vergennes, France's foreign minister, and he felt that he wasn't doing much in Paris. Adams always wanted something to do.

Adams believed that America should rely less on the French. He knew that more money was needed to win the war. Initially acting on his own, Adams sought not only to obtain money but also to establish a relationship between America and the Dutch government.

It would take several months for Congress to formally recognize Adams's position in Holland. In 1781, he became the American minister to the Netherlands. And one year later, he was recognized by the Dutch government.

After he has been in Amsterdam only a few months, Adams writes his fellow diplomat, Benjamin Franklin, about the ups and downs of asking for money. It is interesting that Adams does not admit that France had been loaning money to the patriot cause for quite some time.

> I have felt the mortification of soliciting for money as well as you. But it has been because the solicitations have not succeeded. I see no reason at all that we should be ashamed of asking to borrow money. After maintaining a war against Great Britain and her allies for about six years, without borrowing any thing abroad, when England has been all the time borrowing of all the nations of Europe, even of individuals among our allies, it cannot be unnatural, surprising, or culpable, or dishonorable for us to borrow money. When England borrows, annually, a sum equal to all her exports, we ought not to be laughed at for wishing to borrow a sum, annually, equal to a twelfth part of our annual exports. We may, and we shall, wade through, if we cannot obtain a loan; but we could certainly go forward with more ease, convenience, and safety by the help of one.

The Dutch East India House in Amsterdam with its warehouses and shipyard. The Dutch East India Company was a large trading corporation. Its heydays were from the late 1600s to the middle of the 1700s.

John Quincy and Charles Adams traveled to the Netherlands with their father and went to school there. When Francis Dana, John Adams's secretary, was sent to St. Petersburg, Russia, in 1781 to try to establish relations with the court of Catherine the Great, he took along John Quincy Adams. John Quincy, who spoke fluent French, served as Dana's secretary and translator. That same year, Charles began a long journey home to Massachusetts. This copy of an engraving shows John Quincy Adams as a young man. The original was done while John Quincy Adams was living at The Hague in 1783.

TO JAMES WARREN, SEPTEMBER 6, 1782 (EXCERPT)

Six months after the British surrender at Yorktown, the Netherlands recognized America's independence. Adams was living at The Hague, the seat of the Dutch government. He was hard at work to secure an important loan for America and set up a relationship between the two countries. It didn't take long for his hard work to pay off. Adams secured a loan of more than three million dollars in June 1782. And one month after writing this letter, he signed a treaty of commerce with the Dutch.

Adams wrote constantly about his health during his years in the Netherlands. He was often exhausted and weak and complained of nervous fever and constant stress. As he tells his old friend and fellow statesman, he also felt unappreciated. Yet Adams was extremely proud of his work in the Netherlands and believed it was of great importance for America.

> I hope you have not been all sick, as I have been. I hope you have not all quite so much business as I have to do. At least, I hope it is to better effect, and to more profit both public and private. To negotiate a loan of money, to sign the obligations for

it, to make a thousand visits, some idle, some not idle, all necessary, to write treaties in English, and be obliged to have them translated into French and Dutch, and to reason and discuss every article to – to – to – to – to — &c., &c., &c., is too much for my patience and strength. My correspondence with Congress and their ministers in Europe is a great deal of work; in short, I am weary, and nobody pities me. Nobody seems to know any thing about me. Nobody knows that I do any thing or have any thing to do. One thing, thank God, is certain. I have planted the American standard at the Hague. There let it wave and fly in triumph over Sir Joseph Yorke* and British pride. I shall look down upon the flagstaff with pleasure from the other world.

To Secretary Livingston, December 4, 1782

In late 1782, Adams was back in Paris working with Benjamin Franklin and John Jay to negotiate a preliminary peace treaty with England. This treaty, in which Britain formally recognized America's independence, dealt mostly with national boundaries, debts, navigation of the Mississippi River, fishing rights off the coast of Newfoundland, and British loyalists living in America. For the most part, the war was over and America was independent.

In this letter to Robert R. Livingston, Congress's secretary of foreign affairs, Adams expresses his desire to return home. He is willing to leave his affairs in the Netherlands to Henry Laurens. (It was Laurens who was first assigned to serve America in Holland, but Britain captured him at sea and jailed him in the Tower of London for over a year.) And Adams doesn't think it really necessary to stay in Paris just to sign the "definitive" treaty. Adams recommends his secretary, Francis Dana, for that job.

Sir,—It is with much pleasure that I transmit you the preliminary treaty between the King of Great Britain and the United States of America. The Mississippi, the Western lands, Sagadahoc, and the fisheries are secured as well as we could, and I hope what is done for the refugees** will be pardoned.

As the objects for which I ever consented to leave my family and country are thus far accomplished, I now beg leave to resign

* Yorke was the British minister at The Hague.
** Adams believed that the loyalists should be compensated for the property they lost during the war. In the end, however, it was up to the individual states to compensate them. Most chose not to.

all my employments in Europe. They are soon enumerated, — the first is the commission to borrow money in Holland; and the second is my credence to their High Mightinesses.* These two should be filled up immediately; and as Mr. Laurens was originally designed to that country, and my mission there was merely owing to his misfortune, I hope that congress will send him a full power for that Court.

The commission for peace I hope will be fully executed before this reaches you. But, if it should not, as the terms are fixed, I should not choose to stay in Europe merely for the honor of affixing my signature to the definitive treaty, and I see no necessity of filling up my place; but if congress should think otherwise, I hope they will think Mr. Dana the best entitled to it. With great esteem, I have the honor to be, &c.

John Adams.

France did not take part when the preliminary treaty was drawn up. The preliminary treaty would go into effect—become definitive—only when ratified by Britain and the United States and when Britain and France were at peace. Britain and the United States finally signed the definitive treaty in September 1783 at the same time that Britain, France, and Spain signed another peace treaty ending their hostilities. This print of a painting shows the preliminary treaty of peace being signed in Paris on November 30, 1782.

* "Their High Mightinesses" was the title of the supreme legislature of the Netherlands.

TO JAMES WARREN, AUGUST 27, 1784

Adams *did not* go home, and he *did* sign the definitive peace treaty that ended the Revolutionary War on September 3, 1783. And four days after the signing he was appointed, along with Benjamin Franklin and John Jay, to negotiate treaties of commerce with European countries. (Thomas Jefferson replaced Jay in May 1784. Jay had returned to America and became secretary of foreign affairs after Livingston.) Adams also secured another Dutch loan in early 1784. America was quickly establishing itself as a nation.

If Adams couldn't go home, he could ask his family—finally—to join him in France. In June 1784, Abigail and their daughter—nicknamed Nabby—set sail for England. They landed on July 20, 1784. John Quincy met them there ten days later, and John arrived in early August. Adams and his family then traveled to Auteuil, outside Paris, where they lived for nearly a year.

Adams was glad to be with his family and to be living in the country. It was quite a change from his small apartment at the Hotel du Roi in the middle of crowded Paris where he had lived before. But if Adams is pleased about life in the country, he is upset that he doesn't have enough money to live and entertain well. In this letter to his friend, Adams talks about his role as a diplomat and the need to do a proper job, which requires money.

I received yours of the 29th of June by Mr. Jefferson, whose appointment gives me great pleasure. He is an old friend, with whom I have often had occasion to labor at many a knotty problem, and in whose abilities and steadiness I always found great cause to confide. The appointment of this gentleman, and that of Mr. Jay and Mr. Dana, are excellent symptoms. [Dana had recently been elected to Congress.]

I am now settled with my family at a village called Auteuil, which, although as fine a situation as any in the environs of Paris, is famous for nothing but the residence of the French Swan of the Seine, Boileau, whose house and garden are a few steps from mine. The house and garden where I am, are a monument of the youthful folly of a French nobleman, the Comte de Rouault, who built it at a vast expense, but is now very glad to let it to me at a rent sixteen guineas less than I gave last year for very small and inconvenient apartments at the *Hotel du Roi* in Paris. In house, gardens, stables, and situation I think myself better off than even Dr. Franklin, although my rent is lower. These hills of Auteuil, Passy, Chaillot, Meudon, Bellevue, St. Cloud, and even Mont Martre and Mont Calvaire, although they command the prospect of Paris and its neighborhood, that is, of every thing that is great, rich and proud, are not in my eyes to be compared to the hills of Penn and Neponset, either in the grandeur or the beauty of the prospects.

Congress have mortified me a little by cutting off one fifth of my salary, at a time when the increase of my family rather required an increase of it. The consequence of it must be that I must entertain less company, whereas the interest of the United States requires that I should entertain more. There is not a man in the world less inclined to pomp or to entertainments than myself, and to me personally it is a relief to be excused from both. But if I know any thing in the world, I know that this measure is not for the public good, nor a measure of economy. If there is any body in America who understands economy better than the Dutch nation, I know nothing of either; and their policy is always, upon occasions of consequence, to appoint ambassadors, and even ambassadors extraordinary, as they did at the late peace, my friend Brantzen, with seventy-five thousand guilders to furnish his house and his table, and seventy-five thousand guilders a year to spend in it. In short, that nation which places its own ambassadors at the tail of the whole creation, cannot itself expect to be soon at the head. If this policy do not expose our country to a million insults, and at last compel her by war and bloodshed to consult better her own honor, I am much mistaken. How are we to do? We are to negotiate with all the ambassadors here, that is, we are to be invited to dine to-morrow at a table with three thousand pounds sterling in plate upon it, and next day we are to return this civility, by inviting the same company to dine with us upon earthen ware! I am well aware of the motives to this conduct, which are virtuous and laudable, but we shall find that we cannot keep up our reputation in Europe by such means, where there is no idea of the motives and principles of it, and where extreme parsimony is not economy. We have never been allowed any thing to furnish our houses or tables, and my double capacities have obliged me to furnish myself, both in Holland and France, which, besides exposing me to be unmercifully robbed and plundered in my absence, has pinched and straitened me confoundedly. However, I am the best man in the world to bear it, and so be it.

My affectionate regards to Mrs. Warren and the family.

CHAPTER FIVE

FIRST *U.S.* MINISTER TO GREAT BRITAIN

In truth, I write too much to write well, and have never time to correct any thing.

September 22, 1787

Meeting King George III as America's first minister to Great Britain was an emotional experience for Adams.

To Secretary Jay, June 2, 1785 (Excerpt)

After peace was established in 1783, Adams felt that a minister should be appointed to Great Britain to establish relations between the two countries. Adams wanted the position. In February 1785, just seven months after Abigail and Nabby had arrived from Massachusetts, Adams's wish came true.

Abigail, Nabby, and John left Auteuil for London in May 1785. (John Quincy traveled home then and entered Harvard College the next year as a junior).* The next month, Adams was introduced to the Court of St. James's and to King George III as the first minister to Great Britain. The following day, Adams reports to John Jay, now secretary of foreign affairs, about that historic first meeting.

> Some other gentlemen, whom I had seen before, came to make their compliments too, until the Marquis of Carmarthen** returned and desired me to go with him to his Majesty. I went with his Lordship through the levee room into the King's closet.*** The door was shut, and I was left with his Majesty and the secretary of state alone. I made the three reverences,—one at the door, another about half way, and a third before the presence,—according to the usage established at this and all the northern Courts of Europe, and then addressed myself to his Majesty in the following words:—
>
> "Sir,—The United States of America have appointed me their minister plenipotentiary to your Majesty, and have directed me to deliver to your Majesty this letter which contains the evidence of it. It is in obedience to their express commands, that I have the honor to assure your Majesty of their unanimous disposition and desire to cultivate the most friendly and liberal intercourse between your Majesty's subjects and their citizens, and of their best wishes for your Majesty's health and happiness, and for that of your royal family. The appointment of a minister from the United States to your Majesty's Court will form an epoch in the history of England and of America. I think myself more fortunate than all my fellow-citizens, in having the

* _Thomas also entered Harvard in 1786 as a freshman. His brother Charles was already a student there. John Quincy graduated in 1787, Charles in 1789, and Thomas in 1790._

** _The Secretary of State._

*** _A reception room._

distinguished honor to be the first to stand in your Majesty's royal presence in a diplomatic character; and I shall esteem myself the happiest of men, if I can be instrumental in recommending my country more and more to your Majesty's royal benevolence, and of restoring an entire esteem, confidence, and affection, or, in better words, the old good nature and the old good humor between people, who, though separated by an ocean, and under different governments, have the same language, a similar religion, and kindred blood.

"I beg your Majesty's permission to add, that, although I have some time before been intrusted by my country, it was never in my whole life in a manner so agreeable to myself."

The King listened to every word I said, with dignity, but with an apparent emotion. Whether it was the nature of the interview, or whether it was my visible agitation, for I felt more than I did or could express, that touched him, I cannot say. But he was much affected, and answered me with more tremor than I had spoken with, and said: —

"Sir, — The circumstances of this audience are so extraordinary, the language you have now held is so extremely proper, and the feelings you have discovered so justly adapted to the occasion, that I must say that I not only receive with pleasure the assurance of the friendly dispositions of the United States, but that I am very glad the choice has fallen upon you to be their minister. I wish you, sir, to believe, and that it may be understood in America, that I have done nothing in the late contest but what I thought myself indispensably bound to do, by the duty which I owed to my people. I will be very frank with you. I was the last to consent to the separation; but the separation having been made, and having become inevitable, I have always said, as I say now, that I would be the first to meet the friendship of the United States as an independent power. The moment I see such sentiments and language as yours prevail, and a disposition to give to this country the preference, that moment I shall say, let the circumstances of language, religion, and blood have their natural and full effect."

I dare not say that these were the King's precise words, and, it is even possible, that I may have in some particular mistaken his meaning; for, although his pronunciation is as distinct as I ever heard, he hesitated some time between his periods, and between the members of the same period. He was indeed much affected, and I confess I was not less so, and, therefore I cannot be certain that I was so cool and attentive, heard so clearly, and understood so perfectly, as to be confident of all his words or sense; and, I think, that all which he said to me should at present be kept secret in America, unless his Majesty or his secretary of state, who alone was present, should judge proper to report it. This I do say, that the foregoing is his Majesty's meaning as I then understood it, and his own words as nearly as I can recollect them.

The King then asked me whether I came last from France, and upon my answering in the affirmative, he put on an air of familiarity, and, smiling, or rather laughing, said, "there is an opinion among some people that you are not the most attached of all your countrymen to the manners of France." I was surprised at this, because I thought it an indiscretion and a departure from the dignity. I was a little embarrassed, but determined not to deny the truth on one hand, nor leave him to infer from it any attachment to England on the other. I threw off as much gravity as I could, and assumed an air of gayety and a tone of decision as far as was decent, and said, "that opinion, sir, is not mistaken; I must avow to your Majesty, I have no attachment but to my own country." The King replied, as quick as lightning, "an honest man will never have any other."

TO SECRETARY JAY, DECEMBER 6, 1785 (EXCERPT)

Adams found the job of minister to Great Britain frustrating. Six months after his audience with the king, Adams felt that he was often ignored. In this letter to John Jay, Adams discusses a memorial—or notice—that he plans to present to the British ministry the next day. Knowing that the British will do what they please, he tells Jay that he will leave the country if he does not receive an answer "in a reasonable time in the spring."

In the late 1780s, President George Washington appointed John Jay (above) chief justice of the new Supreme Court.

Adams's notice points to the preliminary and definitive treaties and basically calls for Great Britain to withdraw from several posts it still occupies in the United States. Adams includes the entire memorial in this letter to Secretary Jay.

A MEMORIAL.

The subscriber, minister plenipotentiary from the United States of America, has the honor to represent to the ministry of his Britannic Majesty, that, by the seventh article of the preliminary treaty of peace between his Majesty and the United States of America, signed at Paris, on the thirtieth day of November, one thousand seven hundred and eighty-two, confirmed by the

73

definitive treaty of peace, signed at Paris, on the third day of September, one thousand seven hundred and eighty-three, it was stipulated that his Britannic Majesty should, with all convenient speed, and without causing any destruction, or carrying away any negroes or other property of the American inhabitants, withdraw all his armies, garrisons, and fleets from the said United States, and from every port, place, and harbor within the same, leaving in all fortifications the American artillery that may be therein.

That, although a period of three years has elapsed since the signature of the preliminary treaty, and of more than two years since that of the definitive treaty, the posts of Oswegatchy, Oswego, Niagara, Presque Isle, Sandusky, Detroit, Michillimachinac, with others, not necessary to be particularly enumerated, and a considerable territory around each of them, all within the incontestable limits of the said United States, are still held by British garrisons, to the loss and injury of the said United States.

The subscriber, therefore, in the name and behalf of the said United States, and in obedience to their express commands, has the honor to require of his Britannic Majesty's ministry, that all his Majesty's armies and garrisons be forthwith withdrawn from the said United States, from all and every of the posts and fortresses hereinbefore enumerated, and from every other port, place, and harbor within the territory of the said United States, according to the true intention of the treaties aforesaid.

Done at Westminster, this thirtieth day of November, one thousand seven hundred and eighty-five.

John Adams.

DIARY ENTRY, APRIL 1786 (EXCERPTS)

It took three months for the British ministry to respond to Adams's memorial, and when they did, they did not agree to its terms. Great Britain wanted several states and their citizens to pay their debts to British creditors before they would even consider leaving the Great Lakes forts. Unfortunately for Adams, several states had no intention of paying back British creditors or urging their citizens to do so.

Shakespeare's home, Stratford-upon-Avon, shown about forty years before Adams and Jefferson visited.

Although Adams's political career wasn't going as planned, his personal life was peaceful and happy. In London, he was surrounded by family and friends and stayed in touch with those friends who lived elsewhere. Adams especially enjoyed writing Thomas Jefferson, who had replaced Benjamin Franklin as America's minister to France.

In March 1786, Jefferson arrived at Adams's London home to discuss negotiating treaties with Tripoli, Portugal, and Great Britain. The next month the two diplomats toured several English gardens. Both men were lovers of the land and the week-long trip gave them time to admire the beautiful British countryside.

The following excerpt from his diary reveals Adams's opinion about Stratford-upon-Avon, the village where Shakespeare was born, lived, and was buried. Adams appears to be more interested in Shakespeare's place in history than in the gardens of the area.

Three doors from the inn is the house where he was born, as small and mean as you can conceive. They showed us an old wooden chair in the chimney corner where he sat. We cut off a chip according to custom. A mulberry tree that he planted has been cut down, and is carefully preserved for sale. The house where he died has been taken down, and the spot is now only yard or garden. The curse upon him who should remove his bones, which is written on his gravestone, alludes to a pile of some thousands of human bones which lie exposed in that church. There is nothing preserved of this great genius which is worth knowing; nothing which might inform us what education, what company, what accident, turned his mind to letters and the drama. His name is not even on his gravestone. An ill-sculptured head is set up by his wife, by the side of his grave in the church. But paintings and sculpture would be thrown away upon his fame. His wit, fancy, his taste and judgment, his knowledge of nature, of life and character, are immortal.

The trip also gave Adams time to reflect on America's majestic natural landscape.

It will be long, I hope, before ridings, parks, pleasure grounds, gardens, and ornamented farms, grow so much in fashion in America; but nature has done greater things and furnished nobler materials there; the oceans, islands, rivers, mountains, valleys, are all laid out upon a larger scale.

To the Delegates of Massachusetts in Congress, January 25, 1787

By the beginning of 1787, Adams had had enough and was determined to leave England and return home—as this official letter proves. Adams feels an obligation to tell his fellow statesmen about his decision and counts on their support. Adams's plan was to leave for home as soon as his commission to Britain expired in February 1788.

GENTLEMEN, — I had yesterday the honor of writing to congress my desire and intention to return to America at the expiration of my commission to this Court. I know not the sentiments of my friends in congress, and possibly some of them may wish me to remain longer in Europe. But I beg leave, gentlemen, to signify to you, in this private manner, my fixed resolution to return in all events. Candor requires that I should inform you of this, to prevent you, gentlemen, from compromising yourselves and our state, as well as me. It would expose me to an odium, and do no honor to any member of congress who should vote for me to remain longer in Europe, if I should come home against orders, or without permission.

Let me therefore request the favor of you, gentlemen, and of all the friends I have in congress, to promote my recall, according to the decent plan I have proposed to congress.

I hope the measure will be adopted with perfect unanimity. To be explicit, I am determined to come home, though I should be compelled to do it in an ungracious manner; but I hope this will not be made necessary.

With great respect, &c.
John Adams.

Mather Brown painted this oil portrait of Jefferson in 1786. John Adams owned it in exchange for a Brown portrait of himself.

TO THOMAS JEFFERSON, DECEMBER 6, 1787 (EXCERPT)

As always, John Adams was interested in what was going on in America. The following letter is one of Adams's best statements of his political philosophy. Although he is critical of the U.S. Constitution, Adams still supports it and hopes for its ratification.

Dear Sir, — The project of a new constitution has objections against it, to which I find it difficult to reconcile myself; but I am so unfortunate as to differ somewhat from you in the articles, according to your last kind letter.

You are afraid of the one, I, of the few. We agree perfectly that the many should have a full, fair, and perfect representation. You are apprehensive of monarchy, I, of aristocracy. I would, therefore, have given more power to the president, and less to the senate. The nomination and appointment to all offices, I would have given to the president, assisted only by a privy council of his own creation; but not a vote or voice would I have given to the senate or any senator unless he were of the privy council. Faction and distraction are the sure and certain consequence of giving to a senate, a vote in the distribution of offices. You are apprehensive that the president, when once chosen, will be chosen again and again as long as he lives. So much the better, as it appears to me. You are apprehensive of foreign interference, intrigue, and influence. So am I. But as often as elections happen, the danger of foreign influence renews. The less frequently they happen, the less danger; and if the same man may be chosen again, it is possible he will be, and the danger of foreign influence will be less. Foreigners, seeing little prospect, will have less courage for enterprise. Elections, my dear sir, to offices which are a great object of ambition, I look at with terror. Experiments of this kind have been so often tried, and so universally found productive of horrors, that there is great reason to dread them.

TO SECRETARY JAY, DECEMBER 16, 1787 (EXCERPT)

During the year that he remained in England, Adams accomplished much—personally and professionally. Nabby, who married Adams's secretary, William Stephens Smith, had a son, making John and Abigail grandparents for the first time. He secured another Dutch loan. And he wrote a three-volume work called *A Defence of the Constitutions of Government of the United States of America*, about the country's state constitutions, including his own in Massachusetts.

Mather Brown also painted this portrait of Nabby Adams.

Also, Congress had approved his recall. He and his family would be going home soon.

Writing to a government official, Adams is enthusiastic about the state of the American government and less critical than he was before of the U.S. Constitution.

> The public mind cannot be occupied about a nobler object than the proposed plan of government. It appears to be admirably calculated to cement all America in affection and interest, as one great nation. A result of accommodation and compromise cannot be supposed perfectly to coincide with every one's ideas of perfection. But, as all the great principles necessary to order, liberty, and safety, are respected in it, and provision is made for corrections and amendments, as they may be found necessary, I confess I hope to hear of its adoption by all the States.

TO SECRETARY JAY, FEBRUARY 21, 1788 (EXCERPT)

In late February, Adams bid King George III farewell. Two months later, he and Abigail sailed for home. Adams was fifty-two and had been away for ten years.

Yet Britain and the United States still had not fulfilled their obligations concerning the 1783 treaty, and Adams had been unable to interest the British in negotiating a commercial treaty.

While in London, the Adamses purchased a new home in Braintree. This home is now part of the Adams National Historical Park. G. Frankenstein painted the house in 1849.

Dear Sir, — Yesterday I had my audience of leave of his Majesty. I shall not trouble you with any particulars of the previous steps to obtain this audience (which you know are always troublesome enough), nor with any detail of the conversation, farther than the public is immediately interested in it. The substance of my address to his Majesty was no more than a renewal of assurances, in behalf of the United States, of their friendly dispositions, and of their continued desire to cultivate a liberal intercourse of commerce and good offices with his Majesty's subjects and states, thanks for the protection and civilities of his Court, and good wishes of prosperity to his Majesty, his royal family, his subjects, and dominions. The King's answer to me was in these words. "Mr. Adams, you may, with great truth, assure the United States that, whenever they shall fulfil the treaty on their part, I, on my part, will fulfil it in all its particulars. As to yourself, I am sure I wish you a safe and pleasant voyage, and much comfort with your family and friends."

Adams believed that if another minister were chosen to come to London, he, too, would not be "molded to their [Britain's] views." He also knew that not much would be accomplished without a British minister at congress. He wrote to Jay in the beginning of May 1787, "Let them try the experiment; I dare say they will be disappointed; for, if congress appoints another, he will not be found more to their taste. This country is in a shocking situation; its royal family, its administration, and its opposition, are all such as will never seduce an American from his duty. He will only be shocked at the sight, and confirmed in his natural principles and feelings."

80

CHAPTER SIX

THE COUNTRY'S FIRST VICE PRESIDENT

This Journal is commenced to allure me into the habit of writing again, long lost. This habit is easily lost, but not easily regained. I have, in the course of my life, lost it several times, and regained it as often; so I will now.

July 12, 1796

This statue of John Adams stands in Quincy, Massachusetts.

The Vice President's Speech, April 21, 1789 (Excerpt)

WHEN ADAMS LANDED IN BOSTON, he was hailed a hero. In less than a year, he was elected vice president of the United States. Again, Adams had to leave home—for New York City, the nation's capital.

Upon taking the oath of office on April 21, 1789, Adams covers a lot of ground. He tells his audience that he has never avoided public service, "however dangerous to my reputation, or disproportioned to my talents." He admires the men he is addressing and the "people of America" for the "formation of a national constitution." And he hails Washington as "one, whose commanding talents and virtues, whose overruling good fortune, have so completely united all hearts and voices in his favor."

According to the Constitution, the vice president as head of the Senate could vote on important Senate matters only if there was a tie. At the end of his speech, Adams admits that he has taken part in many political debates but never presided over them. Never one to sit back and "watch" important things take place, Adams would come to find the role of vice president frustrating.

In the summer of 1789, Abigail left Massachusetts to join John at Richmond Hill, a mansion just outside New York City and near Nabby and her family. Adams's home life was far from frustrating.

The inauguration of George Washington took place at New York City's Federal Hall on April 30, 1789. One year later, the capital of the new country moved to Philadelphia.

It is not for me to interrupt your deliberations by any general observations on the state of the nation, or by recommending or proposing any particular measures. It would be superfluous, to gentlemen of your great experience, to urge the necessity of order. It is only necessary to make an apology for myself. Not wholly without experience in public assemblies, I have been more accustomed to take a share in their debates, than to preside in their deliberations. It shall be my constant endeavor to behave towards every member of this most honorable body with all that consideration, delicacy, and decorum, which becomes the dignity of his station and character. But if, from inexperience or inadvertency, any thing should ever escape me, inconsistent with propriety, I must entreat you, by imputing it to its true cause, and not to any want of respect, to pardon and excuse it.

A trust of the greatest magnitude is committed to this legislature, and the eyes of the world are upon you. Your country expects, from the results of your deliberations, in concurrence with the other branches of government, consideration abroad and contentment at home, prosperity, order, justice, peace, and liberty. And may God Almighty's providence assist you to answer their just expectations.

Shortly after becoming vice president, Adams entered into a Senate debate, voicing his opinion about a title for George Washington. Adams believed that the head of the country deserved a grand title and proposed "His Majesty the President." (He also wanted lofty titles for himself and senators.) Others did not agree, and Washington was officially called president. But Adams suffered for his suggestion and became known as "His Rotundity" and the "Duke of Braintree."

A widely known American artist, John Trumbull (1756–1843) is perhaps best known for his four paintings of the American Revolution that hang in the United States Capitol. Trumbull painted this portrait of Adams in 1793.

TO JOHN TRUMBULL, JANUARY 23, 1791 (EXCERPT)

In this letter to John Trumbull, a well-known painter, Adams reveals just how frustrating he finds the job of vice president. Adams tells his friend that he wouldn't mind being a lawyer again.

> The independence of your fame and fortune, and your happiness in private life, are more to be envied than any public office or station. For myself, I find the office I hold, though laborious, so wholly insignificant, and, from the blind policy of that part of the world from whence I came, so stupidly pinched and betrayed, that I wish myself again at the bar, old as I am. My own situation is almost the only one in the world, in which firmness and patience are useless.

Almost three years later, Adams repeats himself in a letter to Abigail.

> My country has in its wisdom contrived for me the most insignificant office that ever the invention of man contrived or his imagination conceived.

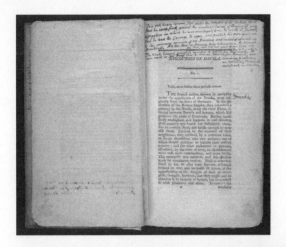

The French Revolution was taking place in 1791. Jefferson favored the Revolution and the overthrow of the king and queen. From 1790–91, Adams wrote "Discourses on Davila," in which he addressed the Revolution and mob violence—what happens when either the people or aristocracies have too much power—and the importance of having one strong leader. Adams's own copy of "Discourses on Davila" (top) is a part of his personal library at the Boston Public Library.

TO THOMAS JEFFERSON, JULY 29, 1791 (EXCERPT)

Vice President Adams was also frustrated by the fact that many people still thought he favored a monarchical form of government—with a king and lords who inherited their positions and an elected House of Commons. Adams did favor a strong central government and would have liked to have seen the president of the United States with more powers. Jefferson, on the other hand, believed in a smaller government with more power given to the states and people. It wouldn't be long before a two-party system based on these differences would form. Jefferson would become a Democratic-Republican (later Republican) and Adams a Federalist.

> If you suppose that I have, or ever had, a design or desire of attempting to introduce a government of King, Lords, and Commons, or in other words, an hereditary executive, or an hereditary senate, either into the government of the United States or that of any individual State, you are wholly mistaken. There is not such a thought expressed or intimated in any public writing or private letter, and I may safely challenge all mankind to produce such a passage, and quote the chapter and verse.

DIARY ENTRY, AUGUST 4, 1796

In 1792, Adams was elected to a second term as vice president. Although he was virtually ignored by Washington during both terms, Adams had some influence in the Senate, casting more than thirty deciding votes, more than any other vice president. And even though he wasn't involved in presidential decisions, his votes supported the Washington administration. Adams was loyal and knew that his role as vice president might eventually lead to the presidency.

In the summer of 1796, Adams was home in Quincy. It seemed likely that Washington would retire, and there was a chance that he would be the nation's next president. But for the time being, sixty-year-old Adams enjoyed the quiet life on his farm and writing in his diary again.

> Of all the summers of my life, this has been the freest from care, anxiety, and vexation to me, the sickness of Mrs. A. excepted. My health has been better, the season fruitful, my farm was well conducted. Alas! what may happen to reverse all this? But it is folly to anticipate evils, and madness to create imaginary ones.

Adams commissioned
Edward Savage to paint
these portraits of George and
Martha Washington in 1790.
They now hang in Adams's
home, part of the Adams
National Historical Park.

CHAPTER SEVEN

THE COUNTRY'S SECOND PRESIDENT

You can't imagine what a man of business I am. How many papers I read and how much I write every day.

April 24, 1797

William Winstanley painted this presidential portrait of John Adams in 1798. Adams was sixty-one when he became president and earned a salary of $25,000.

INAUGURAL SPEECH TO BOTH HOUSES, MARCH 4, 1797 (EXCERPT)

ADAMS RETURNED TO PHILADELPHIA IN DECEMBER and was caught up in the race for president. The most popular candidates were John Adams, Thomas Jefferson, Thomas Pinckney of South Carolina, and Aaron Burr of New York. The race was tight, but Adams officially won in early 1797, beating Thomas Jefferson by only three votes. The president and Jefferson, his vice president, had very different opinions about how the government should run. As a result, Adams would also find the role of president frustrating.

In his first speech as president, Adams outlines the history of the young nation—from the fight for independence to the early forms of government to the coming together of the country under the Constitution. He praises Washington and stresses the importance of a unified country over party politics. He also talks about staying out of foreign affairs, particularly the situation in France. France was also attacking American ships at this time. Involved in a war with England, France felt that America favored England over them. Adams also calls for peace with France.

President Adams sees it as his duty to support the Constitution. Here, he reveals his own personal history and how he came to be president. He also believes it necessary to declare that he is not in favor of monarchy or aristocracy.

Employed in the service of my country abroad, during the whole course of these transactions, I first saw the Constitution of the United States in a foreign country. Irritated by no literary altercation, animated by no public debate, heated by no party animosity, I read it with great satisfaction, as a result of good heads, prompted by good hearts; as an experiment better adapted to the genius, character, situation, and relations of this nation and country, than any which had ever been proposed or suggested. In its general principles and great outlines, it was conformable to such a system of government as I had ever most esteemed, and in some States, my own native State in particular, had contributed to establish. Claiming a right of suffrage in common with my fellow-citizens, in the adoption or rejection of a constitution, which was to rule me and my posterity as well as them and theirs, I did not hesitate to express my approbation of it on all occasions, in public and in private. It was not then nor has been since any objection to it, in my mind, that the

Executive and Senate were not more permanent. Nor have I entertained a thought of promoting any alteration in it, but such as the people themselves, in the course of their experience, should see and feel to be necessary or expedient, and by their representatives in Congress and the State legislatures, according to the Constitution itself, adopt and ordain.

Returning to the bosom of my country, after a painful separation from it for ten years, I had the honor to be elected to a station under the new order of things, and I have repeatedly laid myself under the most serious obligations to support the Constitution. The operation of it has equalled the most sanguine expectations of its friends; and, from an habitual attention to it, satisfaction in its administration, and delight in its effect upon the peace, order, prosperity, and happiness of the nation, I have acquired an habitual attachment to it, and veneration for it.

What other form of government, indeed, can so well deserve our esteem and love?

To Henry Knox, March 30, 1797 (Excerpt)

Most likely, President Adams's first order of business had to do with France—and the possible threat of war.

Not long after the inauguration, former Secretary of War Henry Knox wrote to Adams and recommended sending Thomas Jefferson, the new vice president, to France to settle differences. Knox felt that Jefferson, a past minister to France, was a better choice than Charles Cotesworth Pinckney, the present U.S. minister to France, to do the job. Knox wrote, "It may be suggested that General Pinckney's pride would be hurt by this step. I should believe the contrary. On so momentous a crisis in the affairs of his country, it would be natural for him to be pleased with the countenance of so dignified a person as the Vice-President, and one so much known and respected in France."

Although Adams had sounded out Jefferson about going to France, here he reveals why Jefferson is not a good choice.

I have it much at heart to settle all disputes with France, and nothing shall be wanting on my part to accomplish it, excepting a violation of our faith and a sacrifice of our honor. But old as I am, war is, even to me, less dreadful than iniquity or deserved disgrace. Nothing can be done of much moment, in the way even of negotiation, without the Senate, and nothing else without Congress.

Your project has been long ago considered and determined on. Mr. Jefferson would not go. His reasons are obvious; he has a station assigned him by the nation, which he has no right to quit, nor have I any right, perhaps, to call him from it. I may hereafter communicate to you, what I have never communicated to any other, what has passed upon the subject. The circumstance of rank is too much. We shall never be respected in Europe while we confound ranks in this matter. . . .

If we wish not to be degraded in the eyes of foreigners, we must not degrade ourselves. What would have been thought in Europe, if the King of France had sent Monsieur, his eldest brother, as an envoy? What of the King of England, if he had sent the Prince of Wales? Mr. Jefferson is, in essence, in the same situation. He is the first prince of the country, and the heir apparent to the sovereign authority, *quoad hoc*. His consideration in France is nothing. They consider nobody but themselves.

Before he served as minister to France, Charles Cotesworth Pinckney was a lawyer and officer in the Continental Army. He was also active in South Carolina politics and played a key role at the Constitutional Convention in 1787.

SPEECH TO BOTH HOUSES OF CONGRESS, MAY 16, 1797 (EXCERPT)

Charles Cotesworth Pinckney ended up getting the commission to restore a "mutual confidence between the two republics." But Pinckney had little success. France refused to deal with him, and he was expelled to Amsterdam. In this address to the Senate and House of Representatives, Adams openly discusses France's treatment of Pinckney—and the "suspension" of "diplomatic intercourse"—and the country's attacks on American ships at sea. On one hand, Adams recommends further negotiations and peace with France, but on the other recommends building up the U.S. Navy and U.S. Army. Adams is concerned with protecting the country and preparing for war.

As a Federalist, Adams had recommendations that were at odds with the ideas of the Republicans, the party of Jefferson. The Federalists were pro-British, the enemy of France, while the Republicans favored France.

> I should have been happy to have thrown a veil over these transactions, if it had been possible to conceal them; but they have passed on the great theatre of the world, in the face of all Europe and America, and with such circumstances of publicity and solemnity that they cannot be disguised, and will not soon be forgotten. They have inflicted a wound in the American breast. It is my sincere desire, however, that it may be healed. It is my desire, and in this I presume I concur with you and with our constituents, to preserve peace and friendship with all nations; and believing that neither the honor nor the interest of the United States absolutely forbids the repetition of advances for securing these desirable objects with France, I shall institute a fresh attempt at negotiation, and shall not fail to promote and accelerate an accommodation on terms compatible with the rights, duties, interests, and honor of the nation. If we have committed errors, and these can be demonstrated, we shall be willing to correct them. If we have done injuries, we shall be willing, on conviction, to redress them; and equal measures of justice we have a right to expect from France and every other nation. . . .
>
> While we are endeavoring to adjust all our differences with France by amicable negotiation, the progress of the war in Europe, the depredations on our commerce, the personal injuries to our citizens, and the general complexion of affairs, render it my indispensable duty to recommend to your consideration effectual measures of defence.

To John Quincy Adams, June 2, 1797 (Excerpt)

Like his father, John Quincy Adams devoted his life to his country. In the middle of the 1790s, the younger Adams served as minister to the Netherlands under President Washington. In 1796, Washington appointed him minister to Portugal. In 1797, John Quincy Adams had still not begun his career in Portugal when his father decided to send him to Prussia. Prussia played a key role in the war in Europe. John Quincy's assignment was to renew a treaty with the country and firmly extend Prussia's relations with the United States.

John Quincy Adams was upset with the new appointment and wanted to resign from the diplomatic service. He didn't want people to think he got the assignment because his father was president. However, it seems that President Adams considered his son the best man for this job—perhaps for any diplomatic job overseas.

My Dear Son, — I know not whether I may not have incommoded you, and disappointed your plans, by the alteration I have made in your destination. The mission to Portugal appeared to me to be less important to the United States than a mission to Prussia. The north of Europe, at present, is more interesting to us than the south; the neutral powers of Denmark, Sweden, and Prussia, seem to be naturally more allied, by sympathy, at least, with us neutrals than others, and I thought your talents, sagacity, and industry might be more profitably exerted in collecting and transmitting intelligence of the views and designs of those courts and nations, than they could be in Lisbon, where there will be little to do, that I can foresee, besides sleeping *siestas*. The treaty with Prussia is to be renewed, and after you shall have completed that, you will inform me whether you choose to remain at Berlin, or go to Sweden or Denmark. I would not advise you to make any permanent establishment at Berlin, but keep yourself in a posture to remove to some other court, when you shall have renewed the treaty. . . .

The part which the King of Prussia means to take, either during the war, or at and after the peace, and what his relations are to be in future towards France and England, will be important for us to know. The Emperor of all the Russias, too, and the Emperor of Germany, are important luminaries for the political telescope to observe. In short, what is to be the future system of Europe, and how we best can preserve friendship with them all, and be most useful to them all, are speculations and inquiries worthy of your head and heart. You have wisely taken all Europe for your theatre, and I hope will continue to do as you have done. Send us all the information you can collect. I wish you to continue your practice of writing freely to me, and cautiously to the office of State.

A nineteenth-century wood engraving of John Quincy Adams.

To George Washington, June 22, 1798 (Excerpt)

At the end of May 1797, Adams nominated Charles Cotesworth Pinckney; Francis Dana, his former secretary and chief justice of Massachusetts; and John Marshall, a lawyer from Virginia, to go to France and establish relations between the two countries. It turned out that Dana was too ill and was replaced by Elbridge Gerry, an old friend of Adams. Unfortunately, this mission was unsuccessful. The French refused to recognize the three and even asked for bribe money to enter into an agreement, in what became known as the XYZ Affair.

In less than a year, the United States began an unofficial war with France. The U.S. Navy was established, and the U.S. Army was reinforced with thousands of men. Money was also spent to protect the country's borders. Even though Adams hoped for peace with the European country, he prepared for attacks on sea and land. In June of 1798, Adams writes to George Washington about the possibility of a war on land and asks for his help and support.

Most people favored war with France. Adams was extremely popular at this time.

>   Dear Sir, — I have this morning received with great pleasure the letter you did me the honor to write me on the 17th of this month.

>   Although a visit to the city of Washington would give me great pleasure, and chiefly for the opportunity it would afford me of paying my respects at Mount Vernon, yet I cannot but consider the execution of the plan as very uncertain. I thank you, Sir, for your obliging invitation, and shall certainly wish to spend as much time as possible under the refreshing shade of your vine.

>   The approbatory addresses are very precious to me, as they discover more union among the States, and greater unanimity among the people, than was expected. My administration will not certainly be easy to myself; it will be happy, however, if it is honorable. The prosperity of it to the country will depend upon Heaven, and very little on any thing in my power. I have no qualifications for the martial part of it, which is like to be the most essential. If the Constitution and your convenience would admit of my changing places with you, or of my taking my old

station, as your Lieutenant Civil, I should have no doubts of the ultimate prosperity and glory of the country.

In forming an army, whenever I must come to that extremity, I am at an immense loss whether to call out all the old generals, or to appoint a young set. If the French come here, we must learn to march with a quick step, and to attack, for, in that way only, they are said to be vulnerable. I must tax you sometimes for advice. We must have your name, if you will, in any case, permit us to use it. There will be more efficacy in it than in many an army.

After his presidency ended in 1797, George Washington returned to Mount Vernon, his home in Virginia. He lived there until his death two years later.

In 1796 Adams named his house Peacefield. On September 8, he wrote in his diary, "I think to christen my place by the name of Peacefield, in commemoration of the peace which I assisted in making in 1783, of the thirteen years peace and neutrality which I have contributed to preserve, and of the constant peace and tranquillity which I have enjoyed in this residence." E. Malcolm painted Peacefield in 1798 before Abigail added the 1800 addition.

To Abigail Adams, December 13, 1798

Adams was busy the summer of 1798, preparing the country for war. On July 2, he nominated Washington as commander in chief of the army. Later that month he signed the Alien and Sedition Acts, which dealt with the amount of time a foreigner had to live in the country before becoming a citizen, expelling foreigners considered dangerous, and punishing people who wrote antigovernment material. For Adams, the country needed to take action against its enemies.

Yellow fever was another kind of enemy during the summer of 1798, killing thousands in Philadelphia and other cities. At the end of July, John and Abigail left Philadelphia for their home in Quincy—not only because of the fever epidemic but also to get some peace and relaxation. Unfortunately, their time in Quincy* was far from relaxing. Abigail was deathly ill and John was torn between taking care of her and dealing with the country's undeclared war.

In November, Adams returned to Philadelphia and even more work. He was miserable without Abigail and often complained to her about his situation.

* Part of Braintree (and the place where the Adamses lived) became Quincy in 1792.

My dearest Friend,

Your letters of November 29, December 2 and 3, affect me very tenderly. The low spirits, effects of long and exhausting sickness are apparent; but these are evils of a serious nature. I pray you to banish as much as possible all gloomy thoughts, and be very cautious to avoid every thing which may endanger a return of your old disorders.

To reconcile you to your fate, I have a great mind to give you a detail of mine. A peck of troubles in a large bundle of papers, often in a hand-writing almost illegible, comes every day from the office of ———, office of ———, office of ———, &c., &c., &c. Thousands of sea letters, Mediterranean passes, and commissions and patents to sign; no company—no society—idle, unmeaning ceremony, follies, extravagance, shiftlessness, and health sinking, for what I know, under my troubles and fatigues. You and I seem to have arrived prematurely at the age when there is no pleasure.

All this is not the resignation of Socrates.

I cannot encourage the idea of your coming on to Philadelphia. The horrid roads, and cold, damp weather, would put an end to you. I hope our dear son* will arrive and cheer you up.

I am, with unalterable affection,

J.A.

To Uriah Forrest, May 13, 1799 (Excerpt)

Even though the war with France was popular, Adams decided in early 1799 that he wanted to pursue peace. Acting on his own, Adams nominated William Vans Murray to go to France. His fellow Federalists were appalled, but in the end did not oppose the mission, only the person. Vans Murray, the U.S. minister to the Netherlands, was considered too young. The peace commission would also include Chief Justice Oliver Ellsworth and North Carolina's governor, William Davie.

In March, Adams returned to Quincy and Abigail and stayed until September. Adams would spend a great deal of time in Quincy during his presidency and would be criticized for it. In this letter to Uriah Forrest, a Revolutionary War officer, politician, and former mayor of Georgetown, Adams voices his opinion about his critics.

* This is probably Thomas Boylston Adams, who was on his way home from Europe.

I received on Saturday your friendly letter of 28 April, and I thank you for it, and should be very happy if it were in my power to comply with your advice, not so much on account of any real public utility, as in compliance with what you call the public sentiment. I have reason to believe, however, that this sentiment is chiefly in Philadelphia and Georgetown. "The people elected me to administer the government," it is true, and I do administer it here at Quincy, as really as I could do at Philadelphia. The Secretaries of State, Treasury, War, Navy, and the Attorney-General, transmit me daily by the post all the business of consequence, and nothing is done without my advice and direction, when I am here, more than when I am in the same city with them. The post goes very rapidly, and I answer by the return of it, so that nothing suffers or is lost. . . .

Mrs. Adams, it is true, is better; but she is still in a state so delicate, and has such returns of that dreadful disorder, which kept her on the brink of the grave almost all the last summer, that it would be a presumptuous imprudence, little less criminal than deliberate suicide, for her to attempt to go one hundred miles south of this latitude, before the violent heat of summer shall be passed.

REPLY TO THE ADDRESS OF THE SENATE, ON THE DEATH OF GEORGE WASHINGTON, DECEMBER 23, 1799 (EXCERPT)

In the fall of 1799, Adams returned to Trenton, the temporary capital. Philadelphia was still dealing with the yellow fever epidemic.

Adams had been urgently asked for. The government needed a definite answer to the question, was the country at war or pursuing peace? For Adams, the answer was peace. In October 1799, Vans Murray, Ellsworth, and Davie were sent to Paris to negotiate a peace treaty.

But Adams also promoted defending the country.

Two months later, on December 14, 1799, the country was not prepared for the death of one of its biggest defenders—the commander in chief of the new army. Although Adams often felt jealous of Washington, he recognized his greatness and influence. Here he speaks of that influence in his address to the Senate on December 23. Three days later, Philadelphia, reestablished as the nation's capital, would officially mourn the first president.

Philadelphia, 1800.

In the multitude of my thoughts and recollections on this melancholy event, you will permit me only to say, that I have seen him in the days of adversity, in some of the scenes of his deepest distress and most trying perplexities; I have also attended him in his highest elevation, and most prosperous felicity, with uniform admiration of his wisdom, moderation, and constancy. . . .

For his fellow-citizens, if their prayers could have been answered, he would have been immortal. For me, his departure is at a most unfortunate moment. Trusting, however, in the wise and righteous dominion of Providence over the passions of men, and the results of their counsels and actions, as well as over their lives, nothing remains for me but humble resignation.

His example is now complete, and it will teach wisdom and virtue to magistrates, citizens, and men, not only in the present age, but in future generations, as long as our history shall be read. . . .

To Abigail Adams, November 2, 1800 (excerpt)

Washington, D.C., became the permanent capital of the United States in 1800. It had been designed as the capital with government buildings and a new home for the president. On November 2, Adams writes Abigail about moving into the unfinished President's House. In the letter, he also offers a blessing on the house.

Abigail would join him two weeks later.

> We arrived here last night, or rather yesterday, at one o'clock, and here we dined and slept. The building is in a state to be habitable, and now we wish for your company. . . .
>
> I am very glad you consented to come on, for you would have been more anxious at Quincy than here. . . . Besides, it is fit and proper that you and I should retire together, and not one before the other. Before I end my letter, I pray heaven to bestow the best of blessings on this house, and on all that shall hereafter inhabit it. May none but honest and wise men ever rule under this roof! I shall not attempt a description of it. You will form the best idea of it from inspection.

The east front of the President's House (White House) about seven years after John and Abigail lived there.

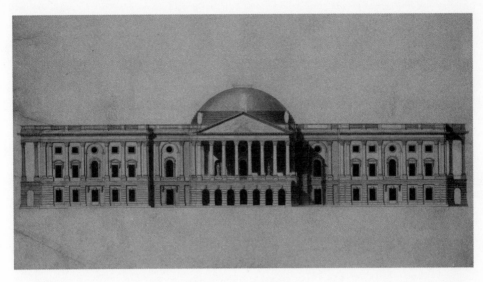

An architectural drawing of the U.S. Capitol in Washington, D.C., created between 1793 and 1800.

SPEECH TO BOTH HOUSES OF CONGRESS, NOVEMBER 22, 1800 (EXCERPT)

Three weeks later, Adams also blesses the new home of the government—the Capitol—in a speech to Congress.

> I congratulate the people of the United States on the assembling of Congress at the permanent seat of their government; and I congratulate you, gentlemen, on the prospect of a residence not to be changed. Although there is cause to apprehend that accommodations are not now so complete as might be wished, yet there is great reason to believe that this inconvenience will cease with the present session.
>
> It would be unbecoming the representatives of this nation to assemble, for the first time, in this solemn temple, without looking up to the Supreme Ruler of the universe, and imploring his blessing.

Adams's greatest triumph came in October 1800, when commissioners Ellsworth, Vans Murray, and Davie established peace with France. Adams received the good news in November.

CHAPTER EIGHT

REJECTION, RETIREMENT, REFLECTION

I . . . write with great difficulty.
December 15, 1809

Abigail Smith Adams (Mrs. John Adams) and *John Adams* by Gilbert Stuart, a well-known American portrait painter, who lived from 1755 to 1828. Stuart began the oil portraits in 1800, when Adams was in his mid-sixties and Abigail in her mid-fifties. He completed them fifteen years later.

To Abigail Adams, Monday, February 16, 1801

IN 1800, ADAMS WAS ALSO RUNNING FOR REELECTION. The election of 1800 is considered by many historians to be one of the fiercest presidential battles between two candidates: Adams and Jefferson.

Newspapers played a big role in the election. Some sided with Adams and his Federalist running mate, Charles C. Pinckney, while others supported Jefferson and his Democratic-Republican running mate, Aaron Burr. But it was the Democratic-Republican press that was the most vocal, pointing out Adams's and the Federalist Party's aristocratic ways and support of big government—taxation, government spending, and restrictions like the Alien and Sedition Acts—over the rights of the common man.

When the electoral votes were counted in December 1800, Adams received sixty-five votes while Jefferson *and* Burr received seventy-three votes each. The final decision was up to the House of Representatives. On February 17, after much debate and backbiting, Jefferson won the election.

The day before, Adams wrote Abigail, who had left Washington earlier, about the final outcome of the election as well as his departure from the presidency. One of Adams's final acts as president was to nominate judges and other officers to serve in the federal government. He also was hosting an official dinner for a group of Indians and dignitaries that evening.

> My dearest friend,
>
> Saturday night, nine o'clock, and not before, I received yours of 13th, and the letter to Thomas with it, brought here no doubt by mistake. I regret very much that you have not a gentleman with you. The skittish young colt with you is always timorous, but no harm will befall you or her, I trust. The weather and roads here on Saturday, Sunday, and to-day, are the finest we have seen this year.
>
> The election will be decided this day in favor of Mr. Jefferson, as it is given out by good authority.
>
> The burden upon me in nominating judges and consuls and other officers, in delivering over the furniture, in the ordinary business at the close of a session, and in preparing for my journey of five hundred miles through the mire, is and will be very heavy. My time will be all taken up. I pray you to continue to write me. My anxiety for you is a very distressing addition to all my other labors.
>
> Our bishop gave us a good discourse yesterday, and every body

inquired after you. I was able to tell them you had arrived on Friday night at Baltimore. I sleep the better for having the shutters open, and all goes on well. I pray God to bless and preserve you.

I give a feast to-day to Indian kings and aristocrats.

Ever

J.A.

On March 4, 1801, inauguration day, Adams cleared out of the President's House at four in the morning. By the time Jefferson took the oath of office at noontime, Adams was well on his way to Quincy—to retirement with his family.

The 1800 election was the last time that a vice president was elected by coming in second. In 1804, with the ratification of the Twelfth Amendment, Americans voted for a president and vice president together. Here, in this late nineteenth-century print, Jefferson travels to his inauguration in 1801.

TO THOMAS JEFFERSON, MARCH 24, 1801 (EXCERPT)

Shortly before he left Washington, Adams learned of the death of his son Charles, a New York lawyer and acute alcoholic. Two other Adams children, Nabby and Thomas, also had difficult adult lives. Nabby's husband could not hold a job, and the family had financial problems. Thomas was an unsuccessful lawyer and heavy drinker. It was only John Quincy who was successful professionally. In 1801, he and his family returned to the United States and would soon find themselves living in Massachusetts.

In this letter to his old friend and new rival, Adams does not appear understanding, but rather disappointed in Charles. Adams did not try to help his son with his drinking problem.

Had you read the papers inclosed, they might have given you a moment of melancholy, or, at least, of sympathy with a mourning father. They related wholly to the funeral of a son, who was once the delight of my eyes, and a darling of my heart, cut off in the flower of his days, amidst very flattering prospects, by causes which have been the greatest grief of my heart, and the deepest affliction of my life. It is not possible that any thing of the kind should happen to you, and I sincerely wish you may never experience any thing in any degree resembling it.

In her book *History of the Rise, Progress and Termination of the American Revolution*, Mercy Otis Warren ridicules Adams.

TO SKELTON JONES, MARCH 11, 1809 (EXCERPTS)

In Quincy, Adams enjoyed working on his three farms and spending time with family and friends. He also found plenty of time to read and write. A year after he returned to Quincy, the sixty-six-year-old began writing his autobiography, which he never finished.

In 1806, Mercy Otis Warren, a well-known author and good friend of Abigail and John, criticized Adams's role as a leader during the Revolution, calling him vain and ambitious. Adams had to defend his reputation. For three years, he wrote letters to the *Boston Patriot* doing just that.

During retirement, Adams often felt neglected and wondered about his place in history. In 1809, historian Skelton Jones began work on a biography of Adams and sent him a list of questions. Adams must have been pleased with Jones's interest. Adams's responses to questions 10, 15, and 17 reveal a lot about him—his physical characteristics, his personality, and his love of books.

> 10. I have one head, four limbs, and five senses, like any other man, and nothing peculiar in any of them.

> 15. My temper in general has been tranquil, except when any instance of extraordinary madness, deceit, hypocrisy, ingratitude, treachery or perfidy, has suddenly struck me. Then I have always been irascible enough, and in three or four instances, very extraordinary ones, too much so. The storm, however, never lasted for half an hour, and anger never rested in the bosom.

> 17. Under my first latin master, who was a churl, I spent my time in shooting, skating, swimming, flying kites, and every other boyish exercise and diversion I could invent. Never mischievous. Under my second master, who was kind, I began to love my books and neglect my sports.

TO DANIEL WRIGHT AND ERASTUS LYMAN, MARCH 13, 1809 (EXCERPT)

Adams, always the patriot, writes to lawyers Wright and Lyman about the importance of an independent and unified country. France and England were at war at this time—and American ships and sailors were caught up in the conflict. President James Madison, a Republican, backed France while Federalists like Christopher Gore, a lawyer and governor of Massachusetts, believed that America should fight France, not Britain. The Federalists even suggested some kind of north–south division of the country based on party differences. In this letter and virtually every other, Adams opposes any division of the country and argues for neutrality between France and

England. Unlike most Federalists, he does not favor Britain over France but wants to hold both at arm's length. Unfortunately, it wouldn't be long until the United States was at war again with Great Britain.

> I am . . . against any division of the Union, by the North River, or by Delaware River, or by the Potomac, or any other river, or by any chain of mountains. I am for maintaining the independence of the nation at all events. I am no advocate of Mr. Gore's declaration of war against France. Knowing, as I do, from personal experience, the mutually friendly dispositions between the people of France and the people of America, Bonaparte out of the question, I shall be very sorry to see them converted into ill will, and old English prejudices revived. Lasting injuries and misfortunes would arise to this country from such a change. I am averse, also, to a war with England, and wish to maintain our neutrality as long as possible without conceding important principles. If either of the belligerent powers forces us all into a war, I am for fighting that power, whichever it may be.

Napoleon Bonaparte served as emperor of France from 1804 to 1814–15.

Benjamin Rush was arguably the most well-known doctor and medical teacher of his day.

TO BENJAMIN RUSH, APRIL 12, 1809 (EXCERPT)

In 1805, Adams resumed his correspondence with Benjamin Rush, a famous Philadelphia physician and treasurer of the U.S. Mint during Adams's administration. He and Rush had been good friends but had grown apart because of distance and differing opinions. Now both were older and enjoyed sharing opinions about religion, politics, and themselves, especially their places in history.

They would exchange letters for four more years, until Rush's death on April 19, 1813.

In the following letter, Adams discusses how hard it is to write his life story. But Adams is not shy about discussing and defending decisions he has made in the past, particularly how he became involved in the fight for independence.

> You advise me to write my own life. I have made several attempts, but it is so dull an employment that I cannot endure it. I look so much like a small boy in my own eyes, that, with all my vanity, I cannot endure the sight of the picture. I am glad you have resolved to do yourself justice. I am determined to vindicate myself in some points while I live. . . .
>
> When I went home to my family in May, 1770, from the town meeting in Boston, which was the first I had ever attended, and

where I had been chosen in my absence, without any solicitation, one of their representatives, I said to my wife, "I have accepted a seat in the House of Representatives, and thereby have consented to my own ruin, to your ruin, and the ruin of our children. I give you this warning, that you may prepare your mind for your fate." She burst into tears, but instantly cried out in a transport of magnanimity, "Well, I am willing in this cause to run all risks with you, and be ruined with you, if you are ruined." These were times, my friend, in Boston, which tried women's souls as well as men's.

I saw the awful prospect before me and my country in all its horrors, and, notwithstanding all my vanity, was conscious of a thousand defects in my own character as well as health, which made me despair of going through and weathering the storms in which I must be tossed.

TO BENJAMIN RUSH, AUGUST 28, 1811 (EXCERPT)

On August 20, 1811, Benjamin Rush writes to Adams about the former president's "integrity" and "name and fame." Rush adds, "I wish you to survive . . . for ages in the veneration, esteem, and affection of your fellow citizens and to be useful to them even in the grave."

Adams is overwhelmed and grateful for his friend's support.

> Your letter of the 20th, my dear friend, has filled my eyes with tears, and, indurated stoic as I am, my heart with sensations unutterable by my tongue or pen; not the feelings of vanity, but the overwhelming sense of my own unworthiness of such a panegyric from such a friend. . . .
>
> Have I not been employed in mischief all my days? Did not the American revolution produce the French revolution? And did not the French revolution produce all the calamities and desolations to the human race and the whole globe ever since? I meant well, however. My conscience was clear as a crystal glass, without a scruple or a doubt. I was borne along by an irresistible sense of duty. God prospered our labors; and, awful, dreadful, and deplorable as the consequences have been, I cannot but hope

that the ultimate good of the world, of the human race, and of our beloved country, is intended and will be accomplished by it. While I was in this reverie, I handed your letter to my brother [in-law] Cranch, the postmaster, of eighty-five years of age, an Israelite indeed, who read it with great attention, and at length started up and exclaimed, "I have known you sixty years, and I can bear testimony as a witness to every word your friend has said in this letter in your favor." This completed my humiliation and confusion.

Your letter is the most serious and solemn one I ever received in my life. It has aroused and harrowed up my soul. I know not what to say in answer to it, or to do in consequence of it.

It is most certain that the end of my life cannot be remote. My eyes are constantly fixed upon it, according to the precept or advice of the ancient philosopher; and, if I am not in a total delusion, I daily behold and contemplate it without dismay.

To Thomas Jefferson, August 24, 1815 (excerpt)

It was Benjamin Rush who suggested that Adams start writing Thomas Jefferson, Adams's old friend and political rival. On New Year's Day in 1812, Adams wrote to Jefferson and Jefferson quickly wrote back. The two former presidents decided to forget that they had been political enemies, and corresponded for almost fifteen years.

Adams and Jefferson discussed everything from religion, politics, education, literature, and history to their personal lives. These letters are considered by many historians to be some of the most important documents in American history.

That our correspondence has been observed, is no wonder, for your hand is more universally known than your face. No printer has asked me for copies, but it is no surprise that you have been requested. These gentry will print whatever will sell; and our correspondence is thought such an oddity by both parties, that they imagine an edition would soon go off, and yield them profits. There has, however, been no tampering with your letters to me. They have all arrived in good order.

To Hezekiah Niles, February 13, 1818 (excerpt)

Adams wrote many people during his retirement. In this letter to Hezekiah Niles, the editor and publisher of the magazine *Niles' Weekly Register*, Adams discusses the American Revolution. Adams wrote often about the history of the country—as early as 1781 with a memorial to the Revolution. Adams wanted others to appreciate that history—write about it—because he thought it was being ignored.

In an 1813 letter, Adams asks, "Can you account for the apathy, the antipathy of this nation to their own history? Is there not a repugnance to the thought of looking back? While thousands of frivolous novels are read with eagerness and got by heart, the history of our own native country is not only neglected, but despised and abhorred."

In this 1818 letter, he takes up the subject again.

> The American Revolution was not a common event. Its effects and consequences have already been awful over a great part of the globe. And when and where are they to cease?
>
> But what do we mean by the American Revolution? Do we mean the American war? The Revolution was effected before the war commenced. The Revolution was in the minds and hearts of the people; a change in their religious sentiments of their duties and obligations. While the king, and all in authority under him, were believed to govern in justice and mercy,

according to the laws and constitution derived to them from the God of nature and transmitted to them by their ancestors, they thought themselves bound to pray for the king and queen and all the royal family, and all in authority under them, as ministers ordained of God for their good; but when they saw those powers renouncing all the principles of authority, and bent upon the destruction of all the securities of their lives, liberties, and properties, they thought it their duty to pray for the continental congress and all the thirteen State congresses, &c.

There might be, and there were others who thought less about religion and conscience, but had certain habitual sentiments of allegiance and loyalty derived from their education; but believing allegiance and protection to be reciprocal, when protection was withdrawn, they thought allegiance was dissolved.

Another alteration was common to all. The people of America had been educated in an habitual affection for England, as their mother country; and while they thought her a kind and tender parent (erroneously enough, however, for she never was such a mother,) no affection could be more sincere. But when they found her a cruel beldam, willing like Lady Macbeth, to "dash their brains out," it is no wonder if their filial affections ceased, and were changed into indignation and horror.

This radical change in the principles, opinions, sentiments, and affections of the people, was the real American Revolution.

By what means this great and important alteration in the religious, moral, political, and social character of the people of thirteen colonies, all distinct, unconnected, and independent of each other, was begun, pursued, and accomplished, it is surely interesting to humanity to investigate, and perpetuate to posterity.

To this end, it is greatly to be desired, that young men of letters in all the States, especially in the thirteen original States, would undertake the laborious, but certainly interesting and amusing task, of searching and collecting all the records, pamphlets, newspapers, and even handbills, which in any way contributed to change the temper and views of the people, and compose them into an independent nation.

The colonies had grown up under constitutions of government so different, there was so great a variety of religions, they were composed of so many different nations, their customs, manners, and habits had so little resemblance, and their intercourse had been so rare, and their knowledge of each other so imperfect, that to unite them in the same principles in theory and the same system of action, was certainly a very difficult enterprise. The complete accomplishment of it, in so short a time and by such simple means, was perhaps a singular example in the history of mankind. Thirteen clocks were made to strike together—a perfection of mechanism, which no artist had ever before effected.

In this research, the gloriole of individual gentlemen, and of separate States, is of little consequence. The *means and the measures* are the proper objects of investigation. These may be of use to posterity, not only in this nation, but in South America and all other countries. They may teach mankind that revolutions are no trifles; that they ought never to be undertaken rashly; nor without deliberate consideration and sober reflection; nor without a solid, immutable, eternal foundation of justice and humanity; nor without a people possessed of intelligence, fortitude, and integrity sufficient to carry them with steadiness, patience, and perseverance, through all the vicissitudes of fortune, the fiery trials and melancholy disasters they may have to encounter.

To Thomas Jefferson, October 20, 1818

During much of 1818, Adams was preoccupied with Abigail and her deteriorating state of health. One week after he wrote Thomas Jefferson, Abigail died of typhoid fever.

In the letter, Adams is also concerned about Jefferson's health. Jefferson had written him on October 7 about being "severely indisposed" with rheumatism. To get well, Jefferson had traveled to warm springs, but the "powerful waters produced imposthume [abscess], general eruption, fever, colliquative [a group of] sweats, and extreme debility." Back home, Jefferson was "getting better slowly."

MY DEAR FRIEND

One trouble never comes alone! At our Ages We may expect more and more of them every day in groups, and every day less fortitude to bear them.

When I saw in Print that You were gone to the Springs, I anxiously suspected that all was not healthy at Monticello.

You may be surprised to hear that your favour of the 7th has given me hopes. "Imposthume, general Eruptions, colliquative Sweats," sometimes and I believe often indicate Strength of Constitution and returning Vigour. I hope and believe they have given you a new Lease for Years, many Years.

Your Letter which is written with your usual neatness and firmness confirms my hopes.

Now Sir, for my Griefs! The dear Partner of my Life for fifty four Years as a Wife and for many Years more as a Lover, now lyes in extremis, forbidden to speak or be spoken to.

If human Life is a Bubble, no matter how soon it breaks. If it is as I firmly believe an immortal Existence We ought patiently to wait the Instructions of the great Teacher. I am, Sir, your deeply afflicted Friend.

John Adams.

Abigail Adams died in this bedroom at Peacefield, which is called the President's Bedroom.

To Robert J. Evans, June 8, 1819 (excerpt)

Adams had servants who worked in his house and in the fields, but he owned no slaves. Slavery *was* allowed in Massachusetts until the early 1780s. While Adams felt strongly about slavery, he, like many other founding fathers, did nothing about it. They were more concerned with setting up a working government. Freeing slaves was not only costly but time consuming.

In 1819, the government was deciding if Missouri should be admitted to the Union as a slave state, expanding slavery to the west. In this letter to Robert Evans, Adams privately calls for the elimination of slavery. The next year, the government would approve the Missouri Compromise, allowing Missouri to become a Slave State on the condition that Maine be admitted to the Union as a Free State.

> The . . . inhumanity, the cruelty, and the infamy of the African commerce in slaves, have been so impressively represented to the public by the highest powers of eloquence, that nothing that I can say would increase the just odium in which it is and ought to be held. Every measure of prudence, therefore, ought to be assumed for the eventual total extirpation of slavery from the United States. If, however, humanity dictates the duty of adopting the most prudent measures for accomplishing so excellent a purpose, the same humanity requires, that we should not inflict severer calamities on the objects of our commiseration than those which they at present endure, by reducing them to despair, or the necessity of robbery, plunder, assassination, and massacre, to preserve their lives, some provision for furnishing them employment, or some means of supplying them with the necessary comforts of life. The same humanity requires that we should not by any rash or violent measures expose the lives and property of those of our fellow-citizens, who are so unfortunate as to be surrounded with these fellow-creatures, by hereditary descent, or by any other means without their own fault. I have, through my whole life, held the practice of slavery in such

abhorrence, that I have never owned a negro or any other slave, though I have lived for many years in times, when the practice was not disgraceful, when the best men in my vicinity thought it not inconsistent with their character, and when it has cost me thousands of dollars for the labor and subsistence of free men, which I might have saved by the purchase of negroes at times when they were very cheap.

American sculptor John Henri Isaac Browere used a plaster cast of Adams's face to create this bust. Browere created busts of many well-known political figures, including Thomas Jefferson.

TO DAVID SEWALL, MAY 22, 1821

Although he had been in pretty good shape during the first years of retirement, Adams's health at eighty-five was failing, especially his hearing and eyesight. He was also greatly affected by the deaths of Abigail, two of his children, and several other family members. But Adams always had time for good friends and was optimistic about the country's future. In this letter to his Harvard classmate, Adams talks about living and dying, the future of the United States, and the new state of Maine, which was no longer a part of Massachusetts.

How do you do? As we have been friends for seventy years, and are candidates for promotion to another world, where I hope we shall be better acquainted, I think we ought to inquire now and then after each other's health and welfare, while we stay here. I am not tormented with the fear of death, nor, though suffering under many infirmities, and agitated by many afflictions, weary of life. I have a better opinion of this world and of its Ruler than some people seem to have. A kind Providence has preserved and supported me for eighty-five years and seven months, through many dangers and difficulties, though in great weakness, and I am not afraid to trust in its goodness to all eternity. I have a numerous posterity, to whom my continuance may be of some importance, and I am willing to await the order of the Supreme Power. We shall leave the world with many consolations. It is better than we found it. Superstition, persecution, and bigotry are somewhat abated; governments are a little ameliorated; science and literature are greatly improved, and more widely spread. Our country has brilliant and exhilarating prospects before it, instead of that solemn gloom in which many of the former parts of our lives have been obscured. The condition of your State, I hope, has been improved by its separation from ours, though we scarcely know how to get along without you.

Information of your health and welfare will be a gratification to your sincere friend and humble servant.

TO JOHN QUINCY ADAMS, FEBRUARY 18, 1825

On February 9, 1825, John Quincy Adams was elected president of the United States, and he immediately wrote his father. It was the first time that a father *and* son served as president of the the country. In this letter, Adams reveals how proud he is of his son's accomplishment.

Before he became president, John Quincy Adams had been a lawyer, diplomat, Harvard professor, state and U.S. senator, and secretary of state under President James Monroe. After John Quincy's presidency, he would continue serving his country as a congressman from Massachusetts—reelected eight times.

My Dear Son,—I have received your letter of the 9th. Never did I feel so much solemnity as upon this occasion. The multitude of my thoughts, and the intensity of my feelings are too much for a mind like mine, in its ninetieth year. May the blessing of God Almighty continue to protect you to the end of your life, as it has heretofore protected you in so remarkable a manner from your cradle! I offer the same prayer for your lady and your family, and am your affectionate father.

John Adams.

John Quincy Adams was married to Louisa Catherine Johnson and had three sons and one daughter.

This funeral wreath was presented to First Lady Louisa Catherine Adams upon the death of her father-in-law, John Adams. It is embroidered with the words: "Presented to Mrs. Adams, Lady of the President of the United States of America, by the Pupils of the Seminary for Female Education at Bethlehem, Pennsylvania. 1826/A.B."

TO JOHN WHITNEY, CHAIRMAN OF THE COMMITTEE OF ARRANGEMENTS FOR CELEBRATING THE APPROACHING ANNIVERSARY OF THE FOURTH OF JULY, IN THE TOWN OF QUINCY, JUNE 7, 1826

A little over a year later, the country was preparing for its fiftieth birthday on July 4, 1826. The town of Quincy looked to John Adams, one of the key figures in the country's beginnings, to play a big part in the celebration. In this dictated letter to John Whitney, chairman of the festivities, Adams excuses himself. Almost ninety-one, Adams was too old to leave his home.

Adams was later asked to give his thoughts about the monumental day. Usually a man of many words, Adams simply said, "Independence forever" —two words that meant so much to him and to his country. They were the perfect motto for the day.

The day would prove monumental in another way. Both Adams and Jefferson were alive to welcome the Fourth, but Jefferson died in the early afternoon and Adams in the early evening. Before he died, Adams uttered, "Jefferson survives." Always competitive with Jefferson, Adams would most likely enjoy knowing that he survived his longtime friend and some-time foe by about five hours.

Your letter of the 3d instant, written in behalf of the commit-tee of arrangements for the approaching celebration of our National Independence, inviting me to dine on the 4th of July next with the citizens of Quincy at the Town Hall, has been received with the kindest emotions. The very respectful lan-guage with which the wishes of my fellow-townsmen have been conveyed to me by your committee, and the terms of affection-ate regard towards me individually, demand my grateful thanks, which you will please to accept and to communicate to your colleagues of the committee.

The present feeble state of my health will not permit me to indulge the hope of participating with more than my best wishes in the joys and festivities and solemn services of that day, on which will be completed the fiftieth year from the birth of the independence of these United States. A memorable epoch in the annals of the human race; destined in future history to form the brightest or the blackest page, according to the use or the abuse of those political institutions by which they shall in time to come be shaped by the *human mind*.

I pray you, Sir, to tender in my behalf to our fellow-citizens my cordial thanks for their affectionate good wishes, and to be assured that I am very truly and affectionately, your and their friend and fellow-townsman.

John Adams.

John Adams's funeral services were held in Quincy, and he was laid to rest in the Hancock Cemetery next to Abigail. Later, Abigail and John (right) were moved to the crypt of the United First Parish Church (below). They are presently there next to John Quincy Adams and his wife, Louisa Catherine.

I am determined no longer to neglect to write to you, lest I should glide away, where there is no pen and ink.

June 2, 1812

The birthplaces of John Adams, left, and John Quincy Adams, below, today.

1735—John Adams is born on October 30 to John Adams (sometimes called Deacon John Adams to set him apart from his son) and Susanna Boylston. He is their first child. The Adams family lives on a small family farm in Braintree, Massachusetts (part of which was renamed Quincy, Massachusetts, in 1792).

1738—Peter Boylston Adams, John's brother, is born.

1741—Elihu Adams, John's youngest brother, is born.

1744—Abigail Smith is born on November 22 in nearby Weymouth, Massachusetts. Her father, the Reverend William Smith, is a Congregational minister. Her mother, Elizabeth Quincy, was born into Braintree's most distinguished family.

1751—Adams enters Harvard College.

1754—The French and Indian War begins in America. The war between the British and French and their Indian allies will become a part of a bigger war—the Seven Years' War—taking place in Europe as well as in European colonies in the Americas, Africa, and Asia.

1755—Adams graduates from Harvard and moves to Worcester, Massachusetts, to teach school.

1756—Adams starts studying to become a lawyer.

1758—Adams is admitted to the Suffolk County bar to practice before the Inferior Court of Common Pleas. Three years later he is sworn in to practice before the Massachusetts Superior Court of Judicature.

1759—Twenty-three-year old John Adams meets fourteen-year-old Abigail Smith.

1760—George III becomes king of Great Britain and Ireland. He will reign until 1820.

1761—Deacon John Adams dies of influenza at the age of seventy. His son inherits the house next to his father's house as well as a barn and several acres of land.

John Adams's law desk (rear) inside the family home. (See bottom photo on page 125.)

1762—Adams's surviving courtship correspondence with Abigail Smith begins.

1763—The Seven Years' War ends with the signing of the Treaty of Paris. The British win the war and take hold of almost all of France's possessions in North America. John Adams begins his career as a published author by writing anonymous essays for Boston newspapers.

1764—The British impose the Sugar Act—a tax on sugar and molasses—on the American colonies in order to help pay for the French and Indian War. John Adams is inoculated against smallpox. John Adams and Abigail Smith are married on October 25, just before his twenty-ninth and her twentieth birthdays. Abigail's father presides over the ceremony, held in her family's home in Weymouth.

1765—In March, Adams becomes the surveyor of highways in Braintree. The Stamp Act, which taxes almost all printed material in the colonies, goes into effect. On July 14, Abigail and John Adams's first child is born. Her name is Abigail, but she is known as Nabby. In late summer and fall, Adams publishes *A Dissertation on the Canon and Feudal Law* in the *Boston Gazette*. He also voices his opinion about the Stamp Act and drafts Braintree's instructions to its legislative representative to oppose the act. His political career is born.

1766—The Stamp Act is repealed. Adams becomes a Braintree selectman.

1767—The Townshend Acts go into effect, placing duties on certain imported goods. The colonists protest by boycotting almost all British goods. On July 11, John Quincy Adams, the Adamses' first son, is born.

1768—The Adamses move into Boston from Braintree. Boston becomes a center of colonial protest. The British army is sent there to establish order. John Adams is offered the position of advocate general, a royal appointment. He refuses. In December, Susanna Adams, the Adamses' second daughter, is born.

1770—In February, Susanna Adams dies. The situation in Boston becomes violent on March 5 when British soldiers kill five colonists. This event becomes known as the Boston Massacre. Adams is elected to the Massachusetts legislature in May. That same month, Abigail gives birth to another son, Charles. In the fall, Adams defends the British captain and soldiers involved in the Boston Massacre.

1771—The Adamses move back to Braintree. John Adams travels to Stafford Springs, Connecticut, for his health.

1772—Thomas, the Adamses' third son, is born on September 15.

1773—The Boston Tea Party takes place in December. Protesting a tax on tea, Massachusetts colonists dressed as Indians dump British tea into Boston's harbor.

1774—The First Continental Congress meets from September to October. John Adams is a delegate from Massachusetts.

1775—Starting in January, Adams writes the Novanglus essays to support the authority of the Continental Congress. They are published in the *Boston Gazette*. In April, battles take place in Lexington and Concord, and the Revolutionary War begins. Adams is a delegate to the Second Continental Congress, serving from May to July and again from September to December. In the middle of June, the Battle of Breed's Hill (also known as Bunker Hill) is fought near Boston. Also in mid-June, in Congress, Adams nominates George Washington to command the Continental Army. Washington takes charge of the troops in Cambridge, Massachusetts, in early July. That same month, John Adams is elected to the Massachusetts Council. In October, he is appointed chief justice of Massachusetts, but his congressional duties keep him from ever serving on the bench. John Adams's youngest brother, Elihu, dies.

1776—Adams serves in the Continental Congress from February to October. In April he publishes *Thoughts on Government*. The Continental Congress adopts the Declaration of Independence on July 4. In September, Adams is part of a peace commission to Staten Island. The Continental Army is victorious at the Battle of Trenton in late December.

1777—The Continental Army is victorious again at the Battle of Princeton in early January. Adams is a delegate to the Continental Congress that meets from January to November. In late summer and early fall, the Continental Army suffers defeats at the Battles of Brandywine and Germantown in Pennsylvania but is victorious at the Battle of Saratoga in New York. In November, the Articles of Confederation are adopted. In late November, Adams, having resigned from Congress, is appointed commissioner to France. In late December, the Continental Army marches to Valley Forge, where they remain until June 1778.

1778—In February, Adams and John Quincy Adams leave for France aboard the ship *Boston*. That same month, France concludes a Treaty of Alliance with America, and France joins the patriot cause. The Adamses land in France in April. In June, the Battle of Monmouth is fought in New Jersey. The outcome is indecisive.

128

John Adams's parents are buried in Hancock Cemetery in Quincy. John and Abigail were first buried there.

1779—In June, Adams, no longer a commissioner, and John Quincy Adams leave France and sail home. In the late summer and early fall, Adams serves in the Massachusetts Constitutional Convention and is responsible for writing almost all of the Massachusetts Constitution of 1780. Also in the fall, Adams is appointed commissioner to negotiate peace and commerce and leaves for France. Two of his sons, John Quincy and Charles, sail with him. They first land in Spain and then travel to Paris.

1780—The Continental Army suffers defeats in Charleston and Camden, South Carolina. Adams travels to Holland to secure a loan. At the end of the year, Adams formally becomes the American commissioner to the Netherlands.

1781—In January, the Continental forces defeat the British at the Battle of Cowpens in South Carolina. In June, Adams becomes part of a new peace commission that is made up of Benjamin Franklin, Henry Laurens, John Jay, and Thomas Jefferson, and in July he briefly returns to Paris to consult with France. The Articles of Confederation are ratified by the states and go into effect. In October, Washington defeats British General Charles, Lord Cornwallis and his troops at Yorktown, Virginia. Cornwallis formally surrenders on October 19.

1782—Adams secures a loan from the Netherlands of more than three million dollars. In October, he signs a commercial treaty with the Netherlands. In November, working with Benjamin Franklin and John Jay, he negotiates and signs the preliminary peace treaty between the United States and Great Britain.

Peacefield today.

1783—Adams, Franklin, and Jay sign the official Treaty of Paris on September 3, thereby ending the Revolutionary War. In October, Adams and John Quincy Adams visit England for the first time.

1784—In May, Adams, Franklin, and Jefferson are commissioned to negotiate commercial treaties with European and North African countries. Adams also secures another loan from the Netherlands. In the summer Abigail and Nabby leave Quincy to join John in Europe.

1785—In February, Adams is appointed the first American minister to Great Britain. He has his first audience with George III in June.

1786—In March and April, Thomas Jefferson visits Adams in London to negotiate treaties, and the two take a short trip through the English countryside. In June, Nabby marries William Stephens Smith in London. In August, Daniel Shays and a group of Massachusetts farmers lead a revolt against high taxes and their state's financial policies brought on by the war (Shays's Rebellion). In August and September, John and Abigail visit Holland.

1787—In April, Nabby gives birth to William Steuben Smith, the Adamses' first grandchild. The Constitutional Convention is held from May to September in Philadelphia. The first volume of Adams's *A Defence of the Constitutions of Government of the United States of America* is published in London. He secures another loan from the Netherlands. In October, Congress grants Adams's request for a recall from all his diplomatic assignments.

1788—In April, John and Abigail leave England for home. Before they leave, John secures another loan from the Netherlands. In June, John and Abigail move into a new house in Quincy that Adams names Peacefield.

1789—Washington is elected president and John Adams vice president of the United States. In April, the new government begins to function under the U.S. Constitution in New York City. In July, a revolution begins in France. It will last for ten years.

1790—Vice President John Adams and Abigail move to Philadelphia, the nation's new capital. Adams begins the serial publication of "Discourses on Davila," his essays criticizing the French Revolution, in Fenno's *Gazette of the United States*.

1791—The Bill of Rights, the first ten amendments to the Constitution, is ratified. Adams stops publishing his "Discourses on Davila."

1792—Washington and Adams are elected to second terms in office.

1793—France is at war with Great Britain and other European powers. Except for a brief period, they will remain at war until 1815.

1794—On November 19, Great Britain and the United States sign the Jay Treaty in England, which settles matters left over from the Revolutionary War. The Federalists support the treaty and a strong relationship with Great Britain. The Democratic-Republicans, however, believe that the treaty is anti-France.

1796—Adams is elected the second president of the United States. Thomas Jefferson serves as vice president.

1797—In April, Susanna Boylston Adams, John Adams's mother, dies. In July, Adams sends his first peace mission to France.

1798—In March and April, Adams releases the XYZ papers, detailing France's attempt to bribe America's peace commissioners and declares a quasi war against France. In May and June, Adams recommends, and Congress establishes, the U.S. Navy. The Alien and Sedition Acts go into effect.

1799—In April, Adams appoints a second peace mission to France but delays sending the commissioners to Europe. In October, over the objections of his cabinet, he dispatches the commissioners. On December 14, George Washington dies at Mount Vernon, his home in Virginia.

1800—On September 30, American diplomats conclude the Convention of Mortefontaine with France, ending the quasi war and formally terminating the Franco-American alliance of 1778. In the fall, Adams and the government move to Washington, D.C., the nation's new capital. He is the first president to live in the President's House, later called the White House. On December 1, son Charles Adams dies. That same month, Adams is defeated by Jefferson and Aaron Burr in his bid for reelection.

1801—In February, Thomas Jefferson becomes the third president of the United States. Aaron Burr is vice president. Before he retires as president, Adams relieves John Quincy Adams of his diplomatic duties in Berlin. In March, Adams decides not to attend the inauguration ceremonies and returns to Quincy to be with family and friends.

1802—Adams begins his autobiography and works on it until 1807.

1804—Thomas Jefferson is elected to a second term. George Clinton is chosen as vice president.

1805—Adams resumes his interrupted correspondence with Benjamin Rush.

The garden outside of Peacefield with Abigail Adams's rose.

1807—Adams begins his controversy with Mercy Otis Warren about her opinions of him in her *History of the Rise, Progress and Termination of the American Revolution*.

1808—James Madison is elected the fourth president of the United States.

1809—Adams writes letters to the *Boston Patriot* about his life and career.

1812—In January, at the urging of Benjamin Rush, Adams resumes his long-interrupted correspondence with Thomas Jefferson. Jefferson is also retired and living at his home, Monticello, in Virginia. In June, the United States is again at war with England. The War of 1812 ends in 1815. James Madison is reelected president.

1813—Nabby dies of breast cancer.

1816—James Monroe is elected the fifth president of the United States.

1818—On October 28, Abigail Adams, seventy-three, dies of typhoid fever at Peacefield. After her death, Adams starts to arrange all his papers—letters, diaries, and important documents.

1820—James Monroe is elected to a second term.

1823—Peter Boylston Adams, John's brother, dies.

1825—In February, John Quincy Adams is elected the sixth president of the United States by the House of Representatives.

1826—On July 4, ninety-year-old John Adams dies just hours after Thomas Jefferson as the country celebrates the fiftieth anniversary of the adoption of the Declaration of Independence.

1828—The bodies of John and Abigail Adams are moved from the Hancock Cemetery in Quincy, Massachusetts, to the Stone Temple (United First Parish Church) in the same town.

1852—The bodies of John Quincy Adams (died 1848) and his wife, Louisa Catherine (died 1852), are placed in a crypt alongside his parents in the Stone Temple (United First Parish Church).

Adams family members pose for a photograph in 1929.

1856—The tenth and last volume of *The Works of John Adams* is published. The editor is Charles Francis Adams, John Adams's grandson. Charles Francis is the son of John Quincy Adams and also a lawyer, politician, and diplomat. In 1861, he became the third Adams, following his grandfather and father, to serve as America's minister to Great Britain.

1946—John Adams's and John Quincy Adams's birthplaces, as well as Peacefield (or the Old House) and the United First Parish Church (also a functioning church), become part of the National Park Service. Four generations of the Adams family lived in the Old House from 1788 until 1927. The fourteen-acre site is known as the Adams National Historical Park.

The police department in Quincy, Massachusetts, celebrates the Adams family.

BIBLIOGRAPHY/ FURTHER RESOURCES

Private letters I have preserved in considerable numbers, but they ought not to be opened these hundred years, and then, perhaps, will not be found of much consequence, except as memorials of private friendship.

March 4, 1815

John Quincy Adams requested that Charles Francis Adams build a safe haven for his books. The Stone Library next to Peacefield was built in 1870 and contains about twelve thousand volumes on history, science, art, music, and theater and represents four generations of the Adams family.

BOOKS

Adams, Charles Francis, ed. *Familiar Letters of John Adams and His Wife Abigail Adams, During the Revolution*. New York: Hurd and Houghton, 1876.

Adams, Charles Francis, ed. *Letters of John Adams, Addressed to His Wife*. 2 vols. Boston: Charles C. Little and James Brown, 1841.

Adams, Charles Francis, ed. *The Works of John Adams, Second President of the United States*. 10 vols. Boston: Little, Brown and Co., 1850–1856.

Akers, Charles W. *Abigail Adams: An American Woman*. 2nd ed., New York: Longman, 2000.

Bohrer, Melissa Lukeman. *Glory, Passion, and Principle: The Story of Eight Remarkable Women at the Core of the American Revolution*. New York: Atria Books, 2003.

Brookhiser, Richard. *America's First Dynasty: The Adamses, 1735–1918*. New York: Free Press, 2002.

Brown, Alice. *Mercy Warren*. New York: Charles Scribner's Sons, 1896.

Chernow, Ron. *Alexander Hamilton*. New York: Penguin Press, 2004.

Diggins, John Patrick. *John Adams*. New York: Times Books; Henry Holt and Co., 2003.

Ellis, Joseph J. *American Sphinx: The Character of Thomas Jefferson*. New York: Alfred A. Knopf, 1997.

Ellis, Joseph J. *Founding Brothers: The Revolutionary Generation*. New York: Alfred A. Knopf, 2001.

Ellis, Joseph J. *Passionate Sage: The Character and Legacy of John Adams*. New York: W. W. Norton & Co., 2001.

Evans, Dorinda. *The Genius of Gilbert Stuart*. Princeton, NJ: Princeton University Press, 1999.

Ferling, John. *Adams vs. Jefferson: The Tumultuous Election of 1800*. New York: Oxford University Press, 2004.

Ferling, John. *John Adams: A Life*. Knoxville: University of Tennessee Press, 1992.

Ferling, John. *Setting the World Ablaze: Washington, Adams, Jefferson, and the American Revolution*. New York: Oxford University Press, 2000.

Grant, James. *John Adams: Party of One*. New York: Farrar, Straus and Giroux, 2005.

Harris, Wilhelmina S. *Adams National Historical Park: A Family's Legacy to America*. Washington, DC: U.S. Department of the Interior, National Park Service, 1983.

Lossing, Benson J. *The Pictorial Field-Book of the Revolution*. 2 vols. New York: Harper & Brothers, 1851.

McCullough, David. *John Adams*. New York: Simon & Schuster, 2001.

Ryerson, Richard Alan, ed. *John Adams and the Founding of the Republic*. Boston: Massachusetts Historical Society, 2001.

Schutz, John A., and Douglass Adair, eds. *The Spur of Fame: Dialogues of John Adams and Benjamin Rush, 1805–1813*. Indianapolis: Liberty Fund, 1966.

Thompson, C. Bradley. *John Adams and the Spirit of Liberty*. Lawrence: University Press of Kansas, 1998.

Thompson, C. Bradley, selector. *The Revolutionary Writings of John Adams*. Indianapolis: Liberty Fund, 2000.

Withey, Lynne. *Dearest Friend: A Life of Abigail Adams*. New York: Simon & Schuster, 2001.

ARTICLES

Brands, H. W. "Founders Chic." *Atlantic Monthly*, September 2003.

"The Danger of Historical Amnesia." *Humanities*, July–August 2002.

Landis, Kathleen. "Mud-Slinging, 1800-Style."*American Spirit*, September–October 2004.

Lord, Mary. "John Adams Slept Here." *U.S. News & World Report*, September 10, 2001.

Rogers, Lisa. "Our Man in Paris." *Humanities*, July–August 2002.

CHILDREN'S MAGAZINES

"The Adams Family." *Cobblestone* 14, no. 9 (November 1993).

"Life and Liberty in Colonial Philadelphia." *Cobblestone* 25, no. 7 (October 2004).

CHILDREN'S BOOKS

Burgan, Michael. *John Adams: Second U.S. President*. Philadelphia: Chelsea House Publishers, 2001.

Fradin, Dennis Brindell. *The Signers: The 56 Stories Behind the Declaration of Independence*. New York: Walker & Co. 2002.

Freedman, Russell. *Give Me Liberty! The Story of the Declaration of Independence*. New York: Holiday House, 2000.

Freedman, Russell. *In Defense of Liberty: The Story of America's Bill of Rights*. New York: Holiday House, 2003.

Harness, Cheryl. *The Revolutionary John Adams*. Washington, DC: National Geographic, 2003.

Hewson, Martha S. *John Quincy Adams*. Philadelphia: Chelsea House Publishers, 2004.

St. George, Judith. *John & Abigail Adams: An American Love Story*. New York: Holiday House, 2001.

Yoder, Carolyn P., ed. *George Washington the Writer*. Honesdale, PA: Boyds Mills Press, 2003.

OTHER MEDIA

Founding Brothers. Produced by Kelly McPherson and directed by Bonnie Peterson and Melissa Peltier. A&E Home Video, 2002. DVD (not rated).

"John & Abigail Adams." PBS: *American Experience*, January 23, 2006.

1776. Produced by Peter Stone and directed by Peter H. Hunt. DVD (rated PG). Columbia Pictures Industries, Inc., 1972, renewed 2002.

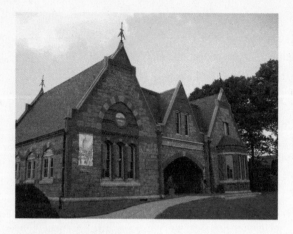

From 1872 to 1908, this building served as the Adams Academy, a boys' school, which was started with a land donation from John Adams. For years afterward, the building was used for a variety of purposes. In 1972, the Quincy Historical Society restored the building and made it its home. Charles Francis Adams, Jr., and other citizens of Quincy, Massachusetts, founded the society in 1893.

PLACES TO VISIT

MASSACHUSETTS

Boston

Boston National Historical Park (www.nps.gov/bost)*

Boston Public Library (www.bpl.org)

Massachusetts Archives and Commonwealth Museum

Massachusetts Historical Society (www.masshist.org)

Massachusetts State House

Museum of Fine Arts (www.mfa.org)

Cape Cod

Sturgis Library, Barnstable (www.sturgislibrary.org)

Quincy

Adams National Historical Park (www.nps.gov/adam)

Hancock Cemetery

Quincy Historical Society (www.quincyhistory.org)

Weymouth

Abigail Adams Birthplace/The Abigail Adams Historical Society (www.abigailadams.us)

NEW YORK

Manhattan

Federal Hall National Memorial (www.nps.gov/feha)

The New-York Historical Society (www.nyhistory.org)

Staten Island

The Conference House (www.theconferencehouse.org)

* *Web sites active at time of publication.*

PENNSYLVANIA

Philadelphia

Atwater Kent Museum of Philadelphia (www.philadelphiahistory.org)

Carpenters' Hall (www.carpentershall.org)

Christ Church (www.christchurchphila.org)

City Tavern (www.citytavern.com)

The Historical Society of Pennsylvania (www.hsp.org)

Independence Hall Association (www.ushistory.org)

Independence National Historical Park (www.nps.gov/inde)

National Constitution Center (www.constitutioncenter.org)

Washington Crossing

The David Library of the American Revolution (www.dlar.org)

WASHINGTON, D.C.

The Library of Congress (www.loc.gov)

U.S. National Archives and Records Administration (www.archives.gov)

The White House

The White House Historical Association (www.whitehousehistory.org)

EUROPE

England

John Adams's Home (Grosvenor Square, London)

France

John Adams's Residence in Auteuil (outside Paris)

The Netherlands

The Hague

The John Adams Institute, Amsterdam

⟞⬦⟝

I can answer but few of the letters I receive, and those only with short scratches of the pen.

May 29, 1818

INDEX

(Page numbers in *italics* refer to illustrations and captions.)

The initials JA and AA in the index stand for John Adams *and* Abigail Smith Adams.

If I had good eyes and fingers, I could write you sheets, if not volumes; but I must soon cease to write at all, even the name of John Adams.

July 13, 1815